Trade in Services and Imperfect Competition

International Studies
in the Service Economy

VOLUME 2

Trade in Services and Imperfect Competition

Application to International Aviation

by

ETHAN WEISMAN
National Centre for Development Studies,
Australian National University,
Canberra, Australia

KLUWER ACADEMIC PUBLISHERS
DORDRECHT / BOSTON / LONDON

Library of Congress Cataloging-in-Publication Data

Weisman, Ethan.
    Trade in services and imperfect competition : application to
international aviation / Ethan Weisman.
        p.   cm. -- (International studies in the service economy; 2)
    ISBN 0-7923-0900-6
    1. Aeronautics, Commercial.   2. Service industries.
3. Competition, Imperfect.   I. Title. II. Series.
HE9777.W45   1990
387.7'4--dc20   90-44395

ISBN 0-7923-0900-6

Published by Kluwer Academic Publishers,
P.O. Box 17, 3300 AA Dordrecht, The Netherlands.

Kluwer Academic Publishers incorporates
the publishing programmes of
D. Reidel, Martinus Nijhoff, Dr W. Junk and MTP Press.

Sold and distributed in the U.S.A. and Canada
by Kluwer Academic Publishers,
101 Philip Drive, Norwell, MA 02061, U.S.A.

In all other countries, sold and distributed
by Kluwer Academic Publishers Group,
P.O. Box 322, 3300 AH Dordrecht, The Netherlands.

Printed on acid-free paper

Printed in the Netherlands

To my family:

L. Y. T. B.

Contents

List of Tables

List of Figures

Acknowledgements

I owe innumerable debts of gratitude to those who have helped me tranform my doctoral thesis into a book. During the research and writing processes I have been guided by some formidable experts. The bulk of the work was completed while a doctoral student at the Graduate Institute of International Studies, Geneva, Switzerland. Beginning with my quest to narrow the topic, I received help from Professors Henryk Kierzkowski and André Sapir and Mr. Brian Crawford. I thank T. F. Davies, Christopher Findlay, Phedon Nicolaides and Harsha Singh for their detailed criticisms and suggestions. In addition I have benefitted from comments made by Svein Andresen, James Brander, Michael Chadwick, John Cuddy, Martin Dresner, Peter Forsyth, Hans Genberg, Anne-Marie Gulde, Tony Kelly, Bruno Lanvin, Dirk Morris, Françoise Nicolas and Harry Stordel. The Centre for Applied Studies in International Negotiations, (CASIN), and the Geneva Trade Policy Dinner Seminars (directed by the late Professor Curzon) deserve my thanks for allowing me to participate in their programs related to trade in services. I also recieved encouragement from the members of the Services World Forum, especially Julian Arkell, Albert Bressand, Orio Giarini, Raymond Krommenacker and Kalypso Nicolaïdis. I also express my gratitude towards St. Hilda's College, Oxford, for hosting me as Visiting Scholar in the summer of 1987. I am grateful to my doctoral dissertation committee, (Professors Henyrk Kierzkowski, (Director), Richard Blackhurst, and André Sapir) for their useful advice. After my doctoral defense I had the pleasure of becoming a post doctoral fellow at the National Centre for Development Studies, Australian National University, Canberra. The assistance given by Helen Hughes, Maree Tate and Rodney Cole at the NCDS is gratefully acknowledged. I am also thankful to Marie Stratta for her friendship and backing which brought this book to fruition. A special note of appreciation goes to my family and friends; their support made this effort possible.

Chapter 1

Aviation, Scope Economies and Services Trade

Aviation policy constantly makes the newspaper headlines with pilot or ground staff strikes, accidents, and mergers. What usually gets omitted from the papers is the role aviation services play in world trade. Overseas travellers choose the airline and routes they wish to fly, but these choices are typically constrained by the regulatory environment and market circumstances existing on those routes. Whether a traveller flies on a national airline or an international competitor determines the pattern of trade in international civil aviation services. This book looks closely at economic factors influencing trade in aviation services to draw lessons for aviation policy, and international trade policy for services. The material in this volume sheds light on important controversies such as: How is trade in aviation services influenced by domestic and international regulation, deregulation and subsidization? What are the impacts of networking on aviation trade? Should aviation services be re-regulated? Does comparative advantage apply to trade in services? What needs to happen in the Uruguay Round of Multilateral Trade Negotiations Group of Negotiations on Services and in future negotiations to promote trade and development, especially for developing countries?

1.1   Liberalization Promotes Scope Economies

The key characteristics of international civil aviation services help yield some interesting conclusions about the economics of aviation, regulation of airlines and other services, and services trade policy. The economic circumstances surrounding aviation and trade in aviation services are similar to those of other service sectors.

The growth of international air transport came rapidly during a turbulent period of world history. The world powers struggled singly and collectively to manage the impacts that this revolutionary technology had on the economic and political structure of the globe. Discord between the great powers resulted in an evolutionary development of the regulation of these services. The bilateral lattice of agreements which exist today create a system of oligopolistic markets stemming from the international regulatory environment.

In the era of deregulation and liberalization this system of markets has adapted. The most dramatic changes have come from the establishment of new networks designed to take advantage of the increased flexibility in the regulatory environment. Improved networking has led to cost savings. It is alledged here that these cost savings are significantly due to economies of scope. This idea is developed more fully throughout the book. The fact that an airline can lower costs by creating a better network of connections means that it has an advantage over competitors that are identical in every other way. Better networks give airlines a competitive edge when competing for market shares.

Regulation of aviation services has not halted completely. Rules still exist that impinge upon a carriers' ability to create an optimal network. Some international or domestic regulations constitute impediments and hence, present obstacles to the efficiency gains associated with improved networks. Clearly the removal of these impediments would allow efficiency gains through better networks. Better networking would make airlines more efficient and promote greater use of international air transportation. The increase in the international trade of aviation services instigates further trade, which would lead to higher standards of living and an improved quality of life globally.

The process of liberalization holds the key to these prospects. The control of regulatory environments stems from a variety of domestic and international sources. Regulators of an individual service sector, such as air transportation, have vested interests and narrow perspectives. Often domestic regulators of services have not taken direct consideration of the effects of their policies on international trade. International agencies which have a particular service sector under their mandate, until recently, have also ignored these impacts. An objective of the present multilateral trade round is to progressively liberalize the economic environment in a way which promotes trade. Recognition of the various agencies and regulators which affect trade must attempt to lead to a harmonization of all levels of regulatory regimes. Enumeration of the trade barriers could assist with this objective. Without conscious and explicit recognition of the rules and conditions which inhibit trade in services the reduction and elimination of these barriers is impossible. The construction of an inventory of this nature could occur within the Uruguay Round of Multilateral Trade Negotiations.

Reiterating and summarizing these key points:

1 Airline behavior resembles an oligopolistic market structure, which is reinforced by the international regulatory environment.

2 Cost savings obtained via networking, (i.e. economies of scope), allow airlines to provide aviation services more cheaply and efficiently. This gives participating airlines an edge when competing for market shares.

3 Regulations at domestic and international levels frequently prevent the creation of optimal networks, limiting the degree of exploitable cost savings.

4 Liberalization of the regulatory environment would improve networks, thereby increasing aviation service efficiency.

5 Liberalization and better networks would also increase the amount of trade in aviation services,(and trade generally), which would increase global living standards.

6 Harmonizing domestic and international regulation of services would promote trade.

7 An inventory approach to regulation and elimination of barriers to trade in services should be agreed during the Uruguay Round of Multilateral Trade Negotiations.

1.2   A Typical Traded Service

International civil aviation services provide an excellent and topical example of traded services. Although not traditionally thought of as a traded activity, this sector exemplifies many of the characteristics common to other services (see Chapter 3). Perhaps the most important feature shared with other services is the amount of regulation to which the sector is subjected. Regulation at domestic and international levels affects the provision of the service output and market structure. Like other services, aviation has recently experienced various degrees of deregulation or liberalization in different parts of the world. Although still highly regulated on most of the international routes, aviation has been deregulated domestically in the United States and has become much more liberalized on several different international routes. The European Community's move towards creating "one market" in 1992 and the impetus provided in the Uruguay Round Group of Negotiations on Services may allow this trend to continue. These experiences have underlined several features of the economic influences of regulation, especially the constraints imposed on networking and market structures.

A model of aviation services is developed and tested in later chapters. This model incorporates the market structure and networking features identified, which aviation services may share with other service sectors. Regulatory interventions imply the need to develop a model which exhibits imperfectly competitive behavior. Recent work expounding the new international trade theory develops the necessary basic tools to construct this model. The results of this exercise gives clear policy directions.

There are a number of good reasons for building and testing this model with application to aviation services. United States aviation policy advisors, during the move towards deregulation in the late 1970's, argued that optimal regulatory policies would permit free entry and exit as well as set safety and pollution standards. The threat of entry would enforce market participants to act in an economically optimal way. Markets would be contested by potential entrants. This is the essence of a regulatory approach based on the theory of contestable markets. Domestic deregulation in the United States led to a dramatic change in the networks of airlines. The new pattern of air transport services moved away from direct, point-to-point, flights and towards a network of connections via hubs-and-spokes. Protagonists of the contestable markets approach initially pointed to aviation as one of the sectors that probably exhibited economies of scope, due to the hubbing-and-spoking networking technique. Economies due to networking are one form of economies of scope. The economies of scope concept has been developed as part of the study of industrial organization. It receives more detailed treatment in the next chapter. Suffice it to state here that economies of scope, in contrast with economies of scale, rely on cost savings due to joint production of differentiated outputs. That is, scope economies require the shared use of inputs across product lines. Industrial organization economists argued that, in theory, hubbing-and-spoking in aviation yields economies of scope. The model developed below tests the importance of these economies of scope in the trade of international aviation services.

Another reason for using aviation services as an example relates to the availability and quality of data. Data on services is appalling. Only recently have efforts been made to assess the contribution of services to employment, growth and trade. On a sectoral level statistics for most kinds of services simply do not exist. In contrast, a long history of data collection exists for aviation services.

Data collection is enhanced by international aviation organizations and regulatory bodies. Relative to other service sectors, international civil aviation services data are easily available and reliable.

1.3 Trade in Services

Although it has gained much attention recently, the topic of international trade in services suffers from a lack of data, theory, and empirical testing. The data problem, albeit significant, remains a long-term concern which will occupy officials for years before more reliable data become available. In the meantime, efforts have already begun to ameliorate the lack of theoretical and empirical work in the area. The present work attempts to make a contribution in these areas.

Standard international trade theory is based on the principle of comparative advantage. For many years the rationale for trade based on this principle has been the well known factor proportions theorem associated with the names of Heckscher and Ohlin. Recently international trade theorists have borrowed heavily from the field of industrial organization to reexplore the consequences for similarly endowed countries of increasing returns to scale production. One of the main conclusions stemming from this interesting work is the fact that there is a theoretical foundation for trade to take place in the absence of different factor endowments between countries as long as economies of scale exist, (see Helpman and Krugman, 1985). This is a significant postulation for trade in services, since many services may exhibit increasing returns to scale in their production.

The point being made here is similar, but nevertheless distinct. That is, there is a theoretical foundation to believe that trade will take place even between countries with identical factor endowments and in the presence of strictly constant returns to scale. Simply put, the presence of economies of scope, provides the rationale for this form of trade. It will be argued that economies of scope is a characteristic of some services and therefore, this rationale embodies another significant motivation for trade in services.

1.4 Trade Policy Relevance

The world economy is undergoing a structural change and services are crucial to this phenonmenon. The most dramatic example of this change is the revolution in computers and their linkages with telecommunications. These technological changes have led to organizational changes and have transformed the global economy. Aviation provides another obvious example where technological change and economic restructuring have made the world seem smaller.

Although the role of the service sector often times has been neglected, (for example, trade theory has not explicitly confronted this area until recently), or regarded as an afterthought (witness the expression "tertiary economy"), recent evidence suggests that services have always played an important part in economic growth and development. Many "industrial" countries must categorize up to two-thirds of their employment in the service sector of the economy. Services and service links with the rest of the economy provide potential for rapid economic growth and employment expansion. Technological advances, particularly in telecommunications, transport and computers, have allowed the service sector to grow at rapid rates. In addition to growth these changes have increased the tradability of services. Whereas many services were difficult, if not impossible, to trade in the past, new technologies have transformed the mode and costs of transactions making trade more viable. For example eletronic data flows have decreased the cost of information and made international sales of databases possible.

In the 1940's attempts to establish the comprehensive International Trade Organization incorporated broad ranging rules for liberalization in services trade, including services involving foreign direct investment or labor movements. Failure to reach agreement on these and other issues (e.g. agricultural trade liberalization) led to the more restrictive and "temporary" General Agreement on Tariffs

and Trade, (GATT). Services trade liberalization was rediscovered in the 1973-79
GATT Tokyo Round discussions on nontariff barriers to trade. With one mi-
nor exception, services were overlooked in the codes developed during the Tokyo
Round.

As far as recent policy issues in international trade in services are concerned,
action initially set in motion by the United States has become embodied in the
Group of Negotiations on Services, (GNS), which falls within the broader context
of the Uruguay Round of Multilateral Trade Negotiations. Increasing recognition
of the growing importance of international trade in services has motivated several
countries to submit national reports on their service sectors to the GATT. In addition, policy actions occuring within the European Community aimed primarily
at creating "one market" by the end of 1992 also focus significant attention on
traded services.

Because of the general dirth of data, theory, and research on this topic, negotiators are often at a relative disadvantage to support their arguments with
factual information. In the chapters which follow several specific trade policy
issues discussed emphasize deregulation and protectionism, (particularly in the
guise of subsidization). It is hoped that this book will contribute to a better
understanding of international trade in services and how policy affects this trade.

1.5   Structure

Background is provided in an historical development of the international regulatory environment and the market conditions regarding international civil aviation
services. The discussion emphasizes the valuable experiences of the United States
and Europe with their moves towards deregulation and liberalization. Another
important feature of aviation services outlined includes an analysis of the applicability of economies of scale and economies of scope. A critical discussion
of previous work on trade in aviation services sets the context for an in depth

examination of the more general issues concerning trade in services.

Armed with the background of facts concerning aviation, concepts differentiating goods from services highlight the prominent characteristics of services. A fresh look at trade in services ensues. Theoretical and empirical analysis are scrutinized so that the development of a model of aviation services can avoid previous shortcomings. Critical features identified for modeling include the abilitiy to capture the market structure caused by regulation and changes in regulation, and the incorporation of economies of scope.

For those readers who are not mathematically or numerically inclined, chapters 5 and 6 can be skipped without too much loss of continuity. The ideas oulined in the early part of the book allow the construction of a formal model of oligopolistic competition which encompasses these features. The model develops the working hypothesis that output is associated with economies of scope and inversely related to the level of competition. The formal exposition explores the implications of the model for trade in international aviation services. It explains the pattern of trade, volume of trade and investigates the trade implications of subsidization and deregulation. The model would remain merely an academic execise unless the working hypothesis can be tested empirically. Careful delineation of the data sources, empirical procedures and results of such a test are designed to rigorously analyze the empirical information and to draw logical conclusions. Exports are statistically positively correlated with the number of passengers flown and empirical observation is consistent with the model. In other words, market structure and economies of scope significantly influence the generation of aviation services exports.

The linkage of exports, via output, to economies of scope and market structure logically leads to a discussion of trade implications. Analysis of the implications for aviation policy focuses on the effects of deregulation and subsidization The policy implications for aviation in Europe receives special attention. Lessons concerning trade policy in aviation services have relevance for other services. A general discussion of the relevance of the findings for the GNS follows. Generalizing from the analysis of international civil aviation services, it is hoped that the implications for trade in services will be used by trade policy-makers and regulators.

Chapter 2

Aviation Facts

This chapter is designed to highlight the features of internationally scheduled aviation services. The following pages are restricted to a brief description of facts and will merely mention whole segments of previous work.[1] The purpose of this exposition is to give the uninitiated reader sufficient information concerning aviation services and hopefully to provide even those familiar with aviation with some new insights.

The next section describes the motivations and manifestations of government regulation in international aviation services. Since regulation predominates, this section identifies the basic market structure and defines the economically pertinent variables. After this description of basic concepts such as entry, output, and prices in international aviation, the subsequent section on deregulation traces recent events in the Unites States and Europe. This is followed by a discussion of the relevance of economies of scale and economies of scope in international aviation services.

---

[1]Those interested in attempts at fuller descriptions should consult the bibliography; Straszheim (1969), Doganis (1985), and Sawers (1987) are excellent background materials.

2.1   Regulated Markets

Not long after the birth of aviation, nation-states claimed that their sovereignty extended to the air space above their territory, by signing the Paris International Air Convention in 1919. This expansion of national jurisdiction inevitably led to governmental controls in air transport. A lattice of bilateral accords subsequently developed until the Second World War. Even before World War II ended, 52 governments gathered to discuss the future of international aviation. Meeting in Chicago in 1944, this multilateral group attempted to find agreement on technical and economic international civil aviation issues. This resulted in the signing of the Convention on International Civil Aviation, (often referred to as the Chicago Convention), which delineated provisions for safety and development, and established the International Civil Aviation Organization (ICAO) in Montreal, Canada. As a part of the United Nations Organization, ICAO is mandated with assisting participants in the aviation sector to develop and maintain operational, technical, and safety standards and practices. Despite this achievement, the Chicago Convention failed to come to terms with the fundamental economic issues involved in international civil aviation, (e.g. pricing policies and traffic rights). The reason for this failure lies with the diametrically opposed positions taken by the two major participants at the Chicago Convention, (the United States and the United Kingdom). The United States, whose aviation sector grew formidably and had better equipment towards the end of World War II, negotiated for an open skies policy. This would have minimized the amount of regulation concerning traffic rights, frequencies and capacities, and fares. On the other hand, the United Kingdom was emerging from World War II with a decimated air transport sector. This led the UK to argue for more controls on traffic, output, and prices. Although another attempt was made to reconcile the differences between these two perspectives in Geneva in 1947, no agreement resulted in either Chicago or Geneva.

Thus, the bilateral system of regulation established before World War II prevailed and developed independently from any multilateral framework. The following subsections take up the issues of traffic rights, frequencies and capacities, and prices. As noted below, traffic rights are decided in state negotiated bilateral air service agreements, (called bilaterals). Frequency and capacity issues are usually resolved between airlines, although they may be arranged within a bilateral and ultimately must be approved by governments. Finally, the International Air Transport Association, (IATA), organizes procedures coordinating prices, however the role played by IATA has diminished over time.

2.1.1 Bilaterals and Traffic Rights

An extremely important feature of international air transport is the ability of an airline to enter a market. Bilaterals regulate entry usually by identifying the number of carriers, routes and kinds of traffic allowed. Although airlines are not listed by name, the phrase "the designated airline" limits services to the carrier appointed by the government. Since most countries only have one carrier, often referred to as the flag carrier or the national airline, designation seldom becomes an issue. Obviously this is not the case where more than one airline exists. Occasionally, more than one designated airline per state may be specified in the bilateral.

In addition, the points or cities served are explicitly enumerated. Different carriers may be designated to different city pairs, if more than one carrier exists in a particular country. Moreover, a specific city-pair's traffic from country A to country B may not be listed as a city-pair for traffic in the opposite direction, (from B to A). Nevertheless, the concept of reciprocity generally rules in the negotiation of bilaterals. In short, all routes (points and direction of traffic) served between the two countries are usually identified in the bilateral.

Passengers flying between the two parties of the bilateral may not fall into the same traffic category. The freedoms of the air define the types of traffic. At the

Chicago Convention the signatories agreed to the first two freedoms: 1) the right to fly over another nation without landing, and 2) the right to land for purely technical reasons (including refuelling). Note that these freedoms do not involve any passenger traffic rights. However, the bilateral grants the two countries basic traffic rights, known as third and fourth freedoms. The third freedom allows a carrier originating in country A to *set down* passengers (and cargo and mail) in country B. The fourth freedom allows a carrier originating in country A to *pick up* passengers (etc.) in country B. Occasionally fifth freedom traffic rights also are negotiated. This would allow a carrier originating in country A to drop off or take aboard revenue traffic between country B and some specified third country, C. In this case country C also would have to agree to this kind of service in its bilaterals with A and B.

Outside the bilateral framework there are two other forms of traffic. For example, the national carrier from country A may combine the fourth and third freedom traffic rights negotiated by A in its bilaterals with both countries B and C. Thus this airline can carry traffic from B to A and then carry it from A to C. Traffic taken from B to C in this manner is referred to as sixth freedom traffic. Even though this kind of traffic is not negotiated within the bilateral, it is highly dependent upon the system of a country's bilaterals. Finally, for the sake of completeness, one should mention cabotage traffic, i.e. traffic flown by a country A carrier between two points within B. This traffic is granted even less frequently than fifth freedom rights, (see Koten, 1987).

2.1.2   Capacity Controls

Capacity, a measure of output, is often measured in available-seat-kilometers (which are the number of seats available on a flight multiplied by air route distance between two airports). This measure must be contrasted with a passenger-kilometer measure of output, which denotes the actual number of passengers carried on a flight times the stage distance flown. The former measure is the subject of concern in bilaterals, while the latter may be determined independently from this regulation. To the extent that the total capacity is specified in a bilateral the upper limit of passenger-kilometers carried by an airline is constrained. Stringent clauses in bilaterals may: specify the capacity between the parties, require that 50 percent of this output be reserved for each national carrier, grant few fifth freedom traffic rights, and/or make "pooling", (see below), mandatory.

Bermuda 1

In Bermuda in 1946 the United States and the United Kingdom agreed to a less restrictive form of bilateral. This type of bilateral, now known as a Bermuda 1, has been used as a prototype across the globe. In terms of traffic rights, a Bermuda 1 grants more fifth freedom rights as long as total capacity relates to end-point traffic, (Dogainis, 1985). More pertinent for the work which follows, there are no frequency or capacity controls. However, if a national carrier feels overwhelmed by the frequency of its competitor, capacity between the countries may come under review. Another characteristic of the Bermuda 1 bilateral was that it condoned airlines use of the International Air Transport Association (IATA) tariff setting procedures, a subject discussed below.

Before turning to the prevalent price-setting mechanisms, it is important to point out a caveat concerning the Bermuda style clauses enshrining the lack of capacity and frequency controls. Despite this apparently liberal attitude towards output, the Bermuda 1 bilaterals do not preclude the use of pooling arrangements.

Pooling

Usually inter-airline pooling agreements concern revenue cost pools or revenue-sharing pools. In a revenue cost pool one airline will serve a market for several other carriers. This carrier will share the costs and revenues with all the parties to the arrangement. This type of pool avoids competition on routes where traffic is too thin to support more than one airline. On the other hand, revenue sharing pools frequently reapportion all revenue among the participants according to the capacity provided in the relevant sector or routes. Without dwelling upon the complexities of this theoretically simple pooling arrangement, suffice it to state that the important factor is the limit, if any, on the transfer of funds between airlines. A lower limit, reduces the relevancy of the pooling agreement and increases the level of competition on the market. Pooling commonly occurs among European nations and can be found among South-East Asian carriers as well, but does not exist on routes involving United States airlines.

2.1.3   Price Coordination

Turn now to the price-setting mechanisms commonly used in internationally scheduled aviation services. As noted above, bilaterals following the Bermuda 1 formula suggest that tariff agreements should use IATA procedures, even though governments reserve their ultimate authority to approve or disapprove these fares. Thus, among the many important coordinating functions that IATA performed as a producers organization, its most prominent function has been to coordinate air fares among airlines. Before 1979 a strict system of price-setting occurred under the IATA tariff conference, which divided the world into three regions, (the Americas, the Pacific-Australasia and a third category covering Europe, Africa and the Middle East). This rigid structure delimited not only fares, which had to be agreed upon unanimously by the members, but also services associated with the transport of passengers. However, by the mid-1970's, this system began to disintegrate because of competitive pressures from non-IATA carriers in South-East Asia and non-scheduled airlines. In 1979 IATA implemented many changes in the tariff coordinating procedures so that the present system is more flexible. Fares between two countries or small geographical regions can be arranged concerning third and fourth freedom carriers, subject of course to government approval. Thus, the necessity of unanimity within the large conferences has been eliminated. The strict rules concerning associated services have practically disappeared. Despite this increased flexibility, air fares coordinated using the new IATA procedures prevail world-wide as the government approved tariffs.

2.2 Deregulation and Liberalization

Recent events have placed the system of regulated aviation services, described in the preceding paragraphs, increasingly under attack. The evolution of these events began primarily in the United States in the 1970's and has spread internationally, especially to Europe. Therefore, a discussion of the international market structure in aviation services is incomplete without a careful look at this trend towards liberalization. The next few pages trace only the most important events and their effects, (see Doganis(1985), McGowan and Trengrove (1986), Morrison and Winston (1986), Pryke (1987), and Sawers (1987)).

The following briefly outlines the effects of deregulation in the United States. Subsequently, agreements among like-minded countries taking a more liberal attitude towards their aviation sectors will be analyzed. Finally, the resulting transmission of liberalization pressure towards the international aviation setting, particularly within the European context is looked at in some detail. This discussion will lead to the need to focus on economic concepts becoming crucial within this liberalizing environment.

2.2.1 The U.S. Experience

The purpose of this section is to motivate the foundations of an economic model of international scheduled aviation services by looking at the experience of the United States of America. To enable the model to handle the characteristics evidenced in air transport, especially for those features particularly relevant to a deregulated or liberalized environment, the U.S. experience with deregulation becomes quintessential. The following paragraphs describe, in the broadest terms, the economic impact of this deregulation up to 1987, (see Bailey, 1985, 1986, Bailey and Graham, 1985, Bailey and Panzar, 1981, Civil Aviation Authority, 1984b, Graham, Kaplan, and Sibley, 1983, International Air Transport Association, 1983, 1984, 1985, 1986, Johnson, 1985, and Kahn, 1982, and 1988). The changes resulting from U.S. deregulation, particularly for consumer prices, efficiency, routes and market structure, will be scrutinized. Their relevance for non-U.S. aviation services will be taken up below.

Deregulation History

Since 1938 the United States Civil Aviation Board (CAB) strictly controlled entry, exit, prices, and several other facets of domestic aviation services. Regulation lasted virtually unchallenged until the mid-1970's, when the Senate and subsequently the CAB began to question many aspects of this regulation. In view of President Carter's impending legislation to deregulate the airlines, the CAB began to loosen its restrictions. In 1977 the CAB loosened its regulatory power by allowing easier route entry and pricing flexibility. With the passage of the Airline Deregulation Act of 1978 the fundamental regulatory environment began to change. In 1982 the CAB's domestic route licensing authority was eliminated freeing route entry and exit. A year later it lost its domestic fares authority and transferred authority over mergers and interlocking arrangements to the U.S. Department of Justice. The CAB was dissolved in 1985 and foreign air transport and subsidy authority moved to the U.S. Department of Transportation.

Price and Entry Effects

The results of price and entry liberalization have had strong and continuing effects on the U.S. air transport sector. The first effect resulting from deregulation was increased competition coming from both new entrants and the adding of new routes by existing airlines. Although incumbent airlines also withdrew from some routes, (and thus some routes obtained less competition), the general level of competition in the USA increased. The consequences of this increased competition were three-fold: lower air fares, increased variety of services, and pressure towards improved efficiency.

Due to the fact that prices became flexible and that many of the new airlines (as well as some of the expanding airlines) were low cost carriers, prices (air fares) dropped markedly, particularly on the routes experiencing more intensive competition (entry).

A second consequence of deregulation was wider variety of services offered. Several of the new low cost entrants provided low cost services as well as charging lower fares. Simplified ticketing and check-in procedures contributed to lower costs, especially on markets with significant amounts of flexible tourist traffic, since these measures generally do not appeal to business travelers. On the other hand, market niches have developed appealing to the customers' preferences for convenience. That is, several airlines have catered to first-class travel by providing high quality services at competitive prices. For these services more comfortable seating configurations and convenient scheduling are priorities. In general, the variety of aviation services has expanded enormously. In addition to the low-cost/high traffic volume and high quality/low density services produced, many different and "in-between" market strategies have been followed in the post deregulation environment.

Naturally a third consequence resulting from the more competitive atmosphere was the pressure towards efficiency. With more competitors, lower prices and wider selection of service quality, many airlines needed to take drastic measures to improve efficiency in order to survive. Two ways airlines found to improve efficiency were through cost cutting and improved networking.

Cost Cutting Cost cutting was most important for incumbent airlines, i.e. those in existence during regulation. With new airlines hiring non-unionized labor several airlines had to make substantial lay-offs and demands for wage decreases to survive and compete. This painful rationalization hit several trunk carriers particularly hard during the early period of deregulation. Other cost saving measures also were implemented. Airlines dropped thin and unprofitable routes that they were required to serve under regulation. In the short-run attempts were made to increase load factors (the percentage of total seats filled by paying passengers) which lowers unit costs.[2] In the longer-run, airlines attempted to reorganize their fleets to handle the traffic on their network more efficiently. The over capacity in both number and size of aircraft generated during the era of regulation plagued several airlines. The significant investment involved in the purchase of a plane, poor resale value due to over capacity, combined with slow depreciation, lengthened the already difficult process of fleet composition adjustment.

Hubbing-and-Spoking   As dramatic as the price declines, and perhaps more important, was the change in airline networking. During regulation considerable amounts of traffic were served by direct point-to-point services. The network of an airline was largely inflexible during this period. Deregulation brought a new environment in which airlines were required to rethink their market strategies and to restructure their network to match this strategy. One small element of this restructuring has already been mentioned above: elimination of thin, unprofitable routes. However, the most significant alteration in airline networking was the development of hub-and-spoke systems to replace the point-to-point services, which proliferated under regulation. Although the concept of a "hub" airport (i.e. a switching point where passengers can make several alternative connections) existed during regulation, the flexibility of entry and exit which came with deregulation allowed its expanded development. In the immediate post-deregulation

---

[2]It is important to remember that fixed costs are high and marginal costs are low in the production of air transportation. For a good discussion of aviation cost structure, see Doganis (1985).

period several carriers developed two hubs, which were thought to be sufficient in number to move traffic across the country. By the mid-1980's this strategy generally has been replaced by the rapid growth in the number of hubs developed by a particular airline.

To appreciate the significance of this change in networking, it will be important to outline the practice and implications of a hub-and-spoke system.[3] A hub airport is simply a central location where several in-coming flights can be connected conveniently on-line (i.e. with a flight from the same company) with several out-going flights within a reasonable period of time. To maximize the number of on-line connections of these "spokes" at a hub, carriers attempt to schedule arrivals from several different places of origin at approximately the same time. While the aircraft are on the ground passengers and baggage are transferred to their connecting flights. Once the transfers are completed the aircraft all take-off at approximately the same time.

There are two main advantages of the hubbing-and-spoking technique. Its use allows tremendous expansion of spoke-to-spoke connection possibilities. Connecting n spokes at a single hub potentially provides $\frac{n(n-1)}{2}$ airports with one-stop service and n additional direct flights, (Civil Aviation Authority, 1984b, p. 52, footnote 34). Another advantage is that, by agglomerating traffic flows into hubs, the increased volume supports more frequent flights.

Wider variety of origin-destinations and increased frequency generally benefits consumers. Passengers enjoy easy on-line connections and simplified baggage transfers under hubbing-and-spoking. Moreover, the multitude of choices and added frequency can more closely conform to consumers' preferences. In fact, greater frequency may compensate for the longer travel time needed for one-stop service compared with a direct flight. In addition to the plain benefits of higher frequency, people traveling in or out of a hub may fly on a larger, more comfortable

---

[3]An excellent treatment of the hubbing-and-spoking phenomenon can be found in Civil Aviation Authority (1984b), appendix three, pages 52-55.

plane. Finally, small communities whose traffic may be too thin to support a direct service may link with destinations via the hub-and-spoke network.

The increased variety of origin-destination pairs by using spokes along with greater frequency maintained by higher traffic volumes enable airlines to obtain a competitive edge. A hub-and-spoke network allows an airline which dominates a hub to attract a disproportionately large share of the connecting markets. This is due to higher frequencies and to the fact that wider selection of destinations publicizes the airlines with travel agents and consumers in the area of the hub. An airline's competitors are at a disadvantage if it connects with its hub at one end of the flight, since numerous connections there enhance the flexibility of the service provided. If the competitor chooses to establish a hub at the same location, he must match the variety and frequency offered or remain at a competitive disadvantage. Another point is that direct flights are discouraged to the extent that frequent connections redirect some of this potential traffic. An important implication concerns the cost savings generated by the hub-and-spoke system. By gathering traffic together on a sector, (station-pair), an airline can lower its unit costs by using larger, more efficient aircraft; increasing load factors; and increasing utilization of aircraft. These economies, which will be explored in more detail below, are limited by the need to shorten flight distances and by the use of constrained and congested hub airports.

The benefits of hubbing-and-spoking and the dramatic adjustments necessitated by this form of networking took time for the domestic U.S. carriers to digest. As noted above, in the transitional stages of deregulation airlines attempted to develop two hubs rather than providing a significant amount of services on all routes. The result was more intensive use of hub airports. Between 1978 and 1986 it was usual for airlines to increase the percentage of flights to or from their two most important hubs from just above 40 percent to over 70 percent, (Jenks, 1986, p.30). In the process of developing only two hubs intensively major airlines lost their markets to competitors. It soon became obvious that two hubs were insufficient. In order to link traffic north, south, east and west, and to avoid the illogical routings required by only two hubs, several new hubs had to be considered. These hubs also created the opportunity to compete with a competitor's nearby hub. This phenomenon caused the proliferation of hubbing across the country.

The Network

Careful planning of the network and hub selection, as well as clearly defining a market strategy, became essential for an airline to survive. Building and protecting a network has taken primary importance in this sector. Since 1978 several airlines have gone bankrupt, yet many airlines were created in the post-deregulation period. Between these extremes, airlines have expanded and shrunk as their ability to build and defend networks varied.

As these transformations took place, linking with hubs became important even for small airlines. It became common for small airlines to establish close relations with larger carriers, feeding their traffic into the larger carrier's hubs. These interlining services allowed the major airlines to effectively expand their network via the linkages with relatively smaller national and regional airlines.[4]

After eight years of adjustment to deregulation, another wave of change hit the air transport sector. In 1986 alone seven large airlines merged with six other large carriers, marking the end of the trend towards lower concentration in overall U.S. aviation, (Sawers, 1987, p. 32). While many of these airlines were absorbed because they could not defend themselves against the intense competition given their high costs and debts, other carriers merged either because their network appeared to complement that of the purchasing airline or because airport facilities available to the absorbed airline were deemed to be valuable assets to the

---

[4]After deregulation airlines which were formerly classified by their certified type of operations, (trunk, local, interstate, commuter, charter), have been redivided by annual turnover. From large to small, airlines are now defined as majors, nationals and regionals; small regionals are known as commuters.

acquiring airline. In other words, takeovers became a useful method of expansion. As already mentioned larger networks lead to higher load factors due to increased on-lining and, therefore, economies for carriers. These network expansions were not limited to domestic travel but saw the hubbing-and-spoking technique work in an international context, allowing domestic passengers to continue on a connecting flight to an international destination. Despite the moves towards a more concentrated sector of the economy, it remains to be shown that any upward trend in prices is due to the exploitation of market power and anti-competitive behavior.

Remaining problems

Two areas of concern with which deregulation did not deal specifically, but which have become extremely important as a result of deregulation and subsequent events, are the constraints of heavily trafficked airports and the development and use of computer reservations systems. Several airports near major U.S. cities are constrained. The slots (landing and take-off times) available are scarce compared with the demands for service. Inadequate rationing of these slots, usually based on historical rights, was one of the rationales behind some mergers. In addition, the development of successful computer reservations systems and their wide-spread use by travel agents has given the airlines which developed these systems a competitive edge. Although there are attempts to correct for this bias, it is not clear that all the advantages gained by the developing company can be neutralized. Both of these areas (and probably several others not listed) provide potential impediments to competition that were not dealt with as part of the deregulation. The U.S. Department of Transportation (DOT) now has the mandate to pursue and resolve these problems to insure a competitive atmosphere. For example, in 1986 the DOT has permitted the buying and selling of slots among airlines. This alleviates but does not resolve the problem of constrained airports.[5]

Obstacles to maintain the level of competition initially experienced after dereg-

---

[5]For some useful policy suggestions see Morrison and Winston (1989).

ulation, such as airport and computer reservations systems constraints, remain in air transport services. However, it appears that the transition towards higher concentration must only alert government officials to these other problems. The reasons why simple concentration does not necessarily lead to abusive monopoly power will be discussed in the last part of this chapter.

Exporting Deregulation

Deregulation in the U.S. did not eliminate all market imperfections in air transport services, yet the professional consensus seems to be that it greatly improved market conditions, increased efficiency, and benefitted both consumers and airlines. Based on the intuition that this would be the result, the U.S. began to pressure the international community to adopt similar measures, especially in international aviation services. An additional motivation comes from the fact that U.S. domestic carriers can use the huge domestic U.S. market to feed a hub with international spokes. Opening up foreign markets, and thereby the creation of more potential spokes, yields advantages to U.S. carriers. Since foreign carriers do not get liberal access to U.S. domestic destinations, non-U.S. carriers are prohibited from reaping these advantages. This pressure manifested itself in two separate ways. First, the U.S. applied direct diplomatic leverage. Second, as a consequence of deregulation U.S. airlines became more powerful and expansive concerning their competition on international routes. The following outlines the renegotiation of some bilaterals and events in Europe, which have in some sense spawned from these pressures.

2.2.2 Renegotiating Bilaterals

U.S. views on deregulation did not remain restricted to domestic routes. A natural consequence of deregulated air transport was the spread of this approach to all connecting transport links. The international context is replete with regulations through bilateral air service agreements. Many of these restrictions have been hard to combat since most countries maintain a single national flag carrier and protection of air transport often is supported by arguments of national security, national pride, and other non-economic factors. The U.S. sought a more liberalized international air transport system by systematically seeking to renegotiate its bilaterals.

One year before the passage of the 1978 U.S. Deregulation Act, the U.S. concluded a new, more liberal form of bilateral with the United Kingdom. The agreement is known as Bermuda 2.[6] Among the innovative concepts that the U.S. brought to the negotiating table, the following were crucial to scheduled services: multiple designation, break of gauge, and country of origin or double disapproval tariffs. All of these ideas work to the advantage of a large traffic generating country served by several carriers. Multiple designation allows the signatories to the bilateral to designate more than one of its airlines to fly a particular route. A break of gauge clause permits an airline to change the size of its aircraft in the other country's territory. For example, passengers continuing on the same flight number may have to change planes as the through service flies to a third country. This would allow an airline to use a smaller plane if traffic on this connection was lower than the flight on the first leg of the journey. Country of origin rules for tariffs gives a party to the bilateral the right to set air fare rules for traffic originating on its soil independently from the wishes of the other party. Similarly, inclusion of an article calling for double disapproval tariffs requires that both parties to the bilateral reject an airline's proposed air fare to invalidate it. All of these measures would liberalize previous bilaterals regulating air transport.

Due to the fact that Bermuda 2 was negotiated before the U.S. had clearly defined its negotiating objectives and undertaken domestic deregulation, the air service agreement was not as liberal as subsequent renegotiated bilaterals with other nations. Despite some limitations on capacity and tariffs, Bermuda 2 in-

---

[6]See Doganis (1985), pp. 56-60, for further analysis.

cluded break of gauge measures and some limited double designations.[7] By early 1978 the U.S. had concluded a much more liberal bilateral with the Netherlands, which was also anxious to expand the competitive potential of the national airline (KLM). Similar bilaterals followed with Belgium and Germany. These included multiple designation and country of origin rules as well as the elimination of restrictions on capacity, frequency and sixth freedom rights. Other conservative European nations have declined to follow suit. However, Israel has concluded an agreement with the U.S. that adds a double disapproval measure to the ingredients found in these renegotiated bilaterals. In addition, the U.S. has renegotiated with Korea, the Philippines, Singapore and Thailand along lines that resemble the Israeli arrangement. The Japanese have also renegotiated with the U.S., but the results were not nearly as liberalizing, except for some limited fifth freedoms. These renegotiations have had spill-over effects with respect to neighboring countries. Given the pressure from the U.S., Canada and West Germany have lifted capacity and frequency controls.

The trend towards more liberalized bilaterals has not spread far. The only other country to systematically follow this movement has been the United Kingdom, (see McGown and Trengrove, 1986, 138-151). After Bermuda 2 the U.K. also renegotiated a bilateral with the Netherlands, culminating in 1984. This bilateral removed capacity and frequency controls and used country of origin tariffs. In 1985 the U.K.-Luxembourg bilateral comprised a double disapproval article on air fares. A parallel bilateral was negotiated with Belgium. Both West Germany and Switzerland obtained bilaterals with the U.K. that were more restrictive than the Luxembourg and Belgian agreements concerning tariff arrangements, but included the free capacity and frequency clauses. The U.K. has also achieved some much less dramatic liberalization with France, Italy and Spain, the more conservative

---

[7]According to Mr. T. F. Davies, Bermuda 1 also included break of guage and multiple designation clauses, which illustrates the point that Bermuda 2 was not as innovative as subsequent bilaterals renegotiated by the U.S.

European countries in international aviation. The push towards greater liberalization in Europe remains the task of the European Community, whose progress is described next. It is certain that the bilateral renegotiations have had a greater impact on the liberalization of European air transport thus far than the European Community's actions.

The effects of renegotiated bilaterals reflected the experience of the U.S. with its domestic deregulation, (Dogainis, 1985, pp. 62-68 and especially McGowan and Trengove, 1986, pp. 134-151). The lack of frequency and capacity controls, as well as multiple designation clauses, encouraged new entry into the liberalized markets. Likewise, country of origin or double disapproval tariffs combined with this increased entry has lowered tariffs. Generally, traffic increased and airlines were forced to look for ways of reducing costs. An interesting phenomenon which occurred on the North Atlantic market as a result of the United States' renegotiations was the significant reduction of the role played by charter air services. Lower scheduled fares drew traffic away from these charters, diminishing their importance.

The renegotiation of bilaterals must not be construed as a panacea for the liberalization of international air transportation. Many international airlines are flag carriers, and as such receive financial support from their government, (if they are not already fully-owned by the government). The ability of the U.S. and the U.K. to renegotiate more liberal agreements results purely from some reciprocation on the part of the other country. It must also be pointed out that the mere inclusion of a multiple designation clause, for example, does not mean that the principle will be called into practice. The practical implementation of liberal articles incorporated into a bilateral is only as liberal as each nation's entry, anti-trust and pricing regulations permit. It appears that the limits of bilateral liberalization by and large have been exploited. General principles for more liberal conduct of international aviation services, as with liberalization negotiations on trade in services, still have to be found.

2.2.3 Towards European Liberalization

A broader method of liberalization than the hesitant renegotiated bilateral is the difficult multilateral agreement. The European Community (EC) has been moving, albeit slowly, in this direction.[8] The discussion which follows outlines the major events leading to the adoption of partial deregulation proposals by EC transport ministers, which went into effect in the beginning of 1988. It appears that a common air transport policy is still a concern for the future. The 1992 target for complete EC competition in air transport services, which fits well with its objective of liberalization of services trade, remains a distant goal.

From its inception, the European Community's 1957 provision for the freedom of movement of services along with the principle of the right of establishment come into direct conflict with the series of highly regulated bilateral air service agreements controlling European air transport.[9] Although initially intended for reform, aviation services provisions within the context of the EC were postponed until the Council could agree on appropriate measures. In the meantime air transport was explicitly exempted from the "freedom to provide services" provision. Nevertheless, exemption from the EC's rules of competition were not explicitly noted. Application could be made of the Treaty of Rome's articles prohibiting agreements which: fix prices, (such as IATA's procedures); limit or control production and markets, (as in bilaterals); or divide markets or sources of supply, (again as in bilaterals). However, during most of the thirty year history of the Community air transport has avoided the scrutiny of these rules.

In 1974 the European Court of Justice found that the general rules of the Treaty of Rome did apply to aviation. By 1979 the Commission produced Mem-

---

[8]This discussion omits the valuable competitive effects of the European charter industry in the North-South leisure travel market. This is one of the features of European aviation which distinguishes it from the U.S. market, where charter flights comprise an insignificant part of the market. For the most part, charters are not subject to bilateral regulations.

[9]An excellent summary of events until 1986 can be found in McGowan and Trengove (1986).

orandum 1. This document took an evolutionary approach to the development of a European air transport policy. None of the proposals, with the exception of a watered-down inter-regional transport measure, was enacted. Preempting previous proposals, the Commission released Memorandum 2 in 1984. These proposals reiterate the clear rejection of a U.S. style deregulation in favor of evolutionary change in the bilateral regulatory system. The Memorandum seeks the eventual application of the Treaty's competition rules to the sector. Many of the proposals reflect the suggestions embodied in renegotiated bilaterals, (e.g. double disapproval and low capacity constraints), as well as the elimination of revenue-pooling and clear identification of state subsidies, which abound in Europe.

Since then the European Court of Justice has delivered two decisions hastening the progress of the EC towards a common aviation policy. In 1985 the Court ruled that the Council had infringed the Treaty by failing to insure the freedom to provide services but that it was up to the Council to decide on a common aviation policy. In the 1986 *Nouvelles Frontières* discounted fares case the Court again found that the Treaty's rules on competition applied to aviation and that it is a violation of an EC Member State's obligations to approve and reinforce air tariffs resulting from agreements which are inconsistent with the Treaty. Effectively this gave power to the Commission to record that Members violate their EC obligations by approving coordinated tariffs. Using this power the Commission took initial steps towards finding a common air transport policy. In 1986 it brought legal proceedings against nine airlines and threatened to take actions which could bring further lawsuits against airlines from travel agents and passengers. With this kind of pressure the Commission finally got transport ministers to adopt mild proposals which came into force in 1988. The adopted proposals allow some limited opportunities to introduce lower air fares and to increase some international competition. The rules also give the Commission more power to investigate airlines and to fine them for anticompetitive practices, (Carey and Wolf, 1987). The EC is still a long way from acheiving full competition by 1992.

2.3   Economies in Aviation

Some of the fears of deregulation or liberalization stem from the belief that economies of scale are present in the production of aviation services. This belief leads to the conclusion that markets will become highly concentrated and airlines will abandon marginal-cost pricing in an attempt to extract monopoly rent, thus resulting in a consumers' welfare loss. The review of recent events has shown that the sector does eventually tend toward higher concentration after deregulation. The development of mega-carriers has not been limited to the United States, as the British Airways-British Caledonian Airways merger demonstrates. This section outlines the evidence of economies of scale in the production of aviation services, which is the basis upon which the fear of monopoly abuse lies. It also explores the evidence concerning another kind of economy in the sector: economies of scope. Before looking at the evidence, however, it is necessary to formally distinguish between these two type of economies. Clarifying these concepts not only allows careful interpretation of the empirical evidence but will also serve as a useful building block for the construction of an appropriate model, the topic of Chapter 6.

2.3.1   Distinguishing Scope from Scale

The following paragraphs define both economies of scale and economies of scope, and show that economies of scope may exist without economies of scale. A constant theme will be to illustrate these propositions with applications to international aviation services.

Economies of scale, simply put, imply that increasing the input factors of production proportionally, (say by λ), will increase output by more than this proportion, (say $\lambda + \alpha$, where $\alpha > 0$). Or, on the cost side, as output rises total cost rises less than proportionally. Average cost will diminish as long as marginal costs are below average costs, thus economies of scale, l, can be measured by:

$$l = \frac{(AC)}{(MC)} = \frac{\frac{TC}{X}}{\frac{\partial TC}{\partial X}} = \frac{\partial X}{\partial TC} \times \frac{TC}{X} = \frac{\partial X}{X} \div \frac{\partial TC}{TC} \qquad (2.1)$$

Note that $l > 1$ implies increasing returns to scale. In other words, the total cost elasticity of output exhibits economies of scale as this ratio exceeds one.

Economies of scope are not the same thing. Panzar and Willig (1981, p. 268) state:

> There are economies of scope where it is less costly to combine two or more product lines in one firm than to produce them separately . . . . Whenever the costs of providing the services of the sharable input to two or more product lines are subadditive (i.e. less than the total costs of providing these services for each product line separately) the multiproduct cost function exhibits economies of scope.

Thus in contrast with economies of scale, economies of scope generally rely on a sharable input and emphasize subadditive costs across product lines.

This distinction may be allusive with regard to airline services. Although passenger-kilometers are considered homogeneous outputs, markets may be divided among different city-pairs. These different markets may be considered different product lines. Note that the definition of different product lines refers to production, not demand, characteristics. Considering the passengers carried on different routes as different product lines and using the hubbing-and-spoking technique could yield economies of scope.

Bailey and Friedlaender (1982, pp. 1026-1028) delineate five different major classes of economies of scope which revolve around the theme of the sharable input. The first class is the classic case of joint production with a sharable input (e.g. sheep yield both wool and mutton). The second class requires the use of not fully utilized indivisible assets (e.g. capital machinery). The third class involves networking, described above, and authors often draw attention to airlines' use of hubbing-and-spoking as an example. The fourth class reuses an input in more than one product line (e.g. recombinable computer files). Finally, the fifth class involves the sharing of intangible assets, or technical knowhow (e.g. engineering plans).

International airline services may exhibit economies of scope in several of these classes. Airports and more specifically an airline's terminal facilities are not fully utilized indivisible assets; networking (i.e. the coordination of hubs and spokes), as already noted, relates to these services; airplanes are reused among different city-pairs[10] and this conforms to the fourth class mentioned above; and fitting into the fifth class, pilots and other technical personnel can operate several different kinds of airplanes and on different sectors.

It is possible to formally distinguish between economies of scope and economies of scale, (see box). Simply having a joint production process does not necessarily imply that either of these economies must exist. Because they are distinct concepts, one may occur without the other. However, economies of scope may imply economies of scale. As Bailey and Friedlaender (1982, p. 1032) put it:

> ...sufficiently strong scope economies can confer scale economies on an entire product set...even if there are constant returns or some degree of diseconomies of scale in the separate products. Also it can be shown that economies of scope and decreasing average incremental cost in each of the product sets together imply overall scale economies.

The following paragraphs explore the applicabilities of these economies to aviation services.

---

[10]There is a fine line between scale and scope concerning the reuse of aircraft. Minimizing ground time permits airlines to gain economies from increased use of their aircraft. To the extent that the outputs are considered a single product line, (i.e. passenger-kilometers), these economies may be considered economies of scale. However, to the extent that outputs are divided into more than one product line, (i.e. passenger-kilometers per city-pair or passenger-kilometers at a particular flight time), these are economies of scope.

Formally Distinguishing Scope from Scale

It is possible to set up a hypothetical situation where cost functions demonstrate economies of scope and not economies of scale. Suppose total costs of outputs X and Y are:

$$TC(X) = cX \tag{2.2}$$

$$TC(Y) = cY \tag{2.3}$$

where c is a constant. Let total costs of production of both X and Y by a single firm be as follows:

$$TC(X,Y) = c(X + Y) - p(XY) \tag{2.4}$$

where p is the coefficient of cost savings associated with production of X and Y and is assumed to be non-negative. By construction economies of scope obtain; equation 2.4 is less than equation 2.2 plus equation 2.3. Note that for marginal costs, $MC_X = MC_Y = c$ and for average costs, $AC_X = AC_Y = c$. The ratio of average costs to marginal cost in both the X and Y activities are equal to one; X and Y are produced separately under constant returns to scale. Moreover, using the definition of product-specific economies of scale and taking average incremental costs as a measure for a multiproduct firm outlined in Bailey and Friedlaender (1982, p. 1030), one finds that the X-product economies of scale, $L(X)$, are:

$$L(X) = \frac{\frac{TC(X,Y) - TC(0,Y)}{X}}{MC_X(X,Y)} \tag{2.5}$$

which means that,

$$L(X) = \frac{\frac{[c(X+Y) - p(XY)] - [c(0+Y) - p(0 \times Y)]}{X}}{c - pY} = 1 \tag{2.6}$$

Thus the firm producing both X and Y exhibits economies of scope but, at the same time, constant returns to scale.

It can be shown that economies of scale can exits in both X and Y industries without the presence of economies of scope. This hypothetical situation can formally be represented by the following equations:

$$TC(X) = cX - l \times X^2 \tag{2.7}$$

$$TC(Y) = cY - l \times Y^2 \tag{2.8}$$

and

$$TC(X,Y) = c(X + Y) - l \times (X^2 + Y^2) \tag{2.9}$$

In this case the first two equations sum to the third and no economies of scope obtain. However, the average costs of these industries exceed marginal costs, ($MC_i = c - 2l \times i$, $AC_i = c - l \times i$, and $\frac{AC_i}{MC_i} > 1$, where $i = X, Y$). Economies of scale are present in single product production. Finally, product-specific economies of scale are also present. Equation 2.5 in this case yields:

$$L(X) = \frac{\frac{[c(X+Y) - l \times (X^2 + Y^2)] - [cY - l \times Y^2]}{X}}{c - 2l \times X} > 1 \tag{2.10}$$

Thus a firm producing both outputs exhibits economies of scale but not economies of scope.

2.3.2   Looking for Economies of Scale

There are really two distinct contexts for economies of scale: the city-pair and across an airline's operations. It is confusing to read about aviation economics with regard to economies of scale. Authors are prone to categorically state that these economies exist or are lacking while ignoring or casually observing the evidence. Early studies which ignored the effects of shorter flight distances and lower densities, (characterizing the routes generally served by smaller airlines), led some writers to conclude that size affects costs.

With the technological innovation of wide-bodied aircraft it is easy to imagine the possibility of economies of scale on a single route. The Graham, Kaplan, Sibley (1983) study argues that economies of scale exist for airlines on a single route basis, since the use of large aircraft at higher load factors reduces costs. However, these alleged economies of scale may really reflect a change in the production function, since the technology used is altered. Therefore, even this claim of economies of scale is questionable.[11] Stressing that statistical evidence of city-pair economies of scale is lacking, White (1979) underlines the casual empirical observation that these economies cannot be relevant across all ranges of output. Most importantly, economies of scale on a particular route implies nothing for the possibility of scale economies across an airline's network.

One of the earliest economic studies of international aviation (Strazheim, 1962) concluded that economies of scale were not present across an airline's operations. White (1979) noted that, in addition to Strazheim's work, eleven other analyses

---

[11]Mr. T. F. Davies makes the same point in correspondence with the author using different reasoning:

> It should be recognized that if high load factors cause a reduction in seat access (i.e. fewer seats available for on-demand purchase) then this represents a reduction in product standard which is offered. In these circumstances lower costs are not economies of scale but a change in the production function.

(primarily of U.S. airlines) had similar findings. In short, "economies of scale are negligible or non-existent at the overall firm level", (White, 1979, p. 564).

Recent research concurs with these conclusions. The U.K. Civil Aviation Authority (1984) report agrees that there are no cost advantages attributable solely to the size of an airline in the U.S. and implies that this applies to the U.K. equally well. The careful work of Caves, Christensen, and Tretheway (1984) supports these findings, adding that different kind of economies are derived from increasing the density of traffic on a network. Finally, Sawers (1986) draws the same results from a simplified analysis by showing that the size of an airline's operations and profit margins are not related in a systematic way.

2.3.3 The Economies of Scope Hypothesis

It has been hinted that despite the lack of evidence of economies of scale, aviation services are subject to economies related to the building of a network. These economies are are closely associated with the hubbing-and-spoking phenomenon. The CAA findings based on interviews and reports from aviation producers states that in the U.S. there is a belief that route density and network integration provides economies and again implies that these economies are relevant for U.K. scheduled services. Johnson (1985) confirms this belief, by showing empirically that the success of an entering airline in the early stages of U.S. deregulation depended upon the way in which the new route fit into an airline's previously established network and the degree of intraline feeding resulting from this structure. As already mentioned, Caves, Christensen, Tretheway (1984) provide statistical evidence for this belief. This is not surprising. The discussion of hubbing-and-spoking above witnessed the increased density resulting from this new networking fabric. The empirical evidence of Bailey, Graham, and Kaplan (1985) that increasing the amount of continuing passengers, (i.e. on-lining),allowed airlines to improve their load factors combined with the fact that higher load factors lowers unit costs, implies that the networking technique leads to economies. These economies have been labeled economies of scope, (see Panzar and Willig, 1981, Bailey and Friedlaender, 1982, and Baumol, Panzar and Willig, 1982). A recent paper by G. Bittlingmayer (1985) provides a theoretical framework exhibiting economies of scope in U.S. aviation as a result of hubbing-and-spoking. Explicit empirical evidence of economies of scope in international aviation has yet to appear and is one of the main objectives of Chapter 7.

2.4 Summary

The post World War II development of a latice of bilateral air service agreements effectively regulated entry, output and prices outside of a multilateral framework. Since the late 1970's a trend towards more liberalized control of internationally scheduled aviation services has prevailed. The domestic U.S. experience and the results found on particular sectors where bilaterals have become less restrictive leads to similar conclusions. Liberalization has generally increased entry, improved the range of service quality, lowered prices and put pressure towards efficiency. A notable change in networking also has occurred in the U.S. case of deregulation. Given the freedom to do so, airlines have chosen to restructure their networks into hubs-and-spokes, resulting in benefits for consumers and producers. Hubbing-and-spoking and the economies derived allows an airline to increase output of passenger services; this has been key to carriers' survivability and success. All those passengers wanting to get from the hub to a particular spoke are agglomerated with all the passengers from the various other spokes that wish to fly to that same destination. The desire to arrive at that spoke is served via a spoke-hub-spoke one-stop service. Traffic might otherwise be too thin to support this traffic and/or flight frequencies might be too sparse to allow for convenient travel. The hub-and-spoke network raises densities on all routes by accumulating traffic in this way. Combining possible economies of larger aircraft on a route level with the increased density caused by hubbing-and-spoking yields economies of scope. The economies derived from this new networking reflect economies of scope and not economies of scale. Without the networking technique mere size of an airline cannot yield the scale economies intuitively sought by an observer of aviation economics. Empirical evidence on aviation services shows either negligible or non-existent economies of scale. Chapter 7 provides evidence of economies of scope in international aviation.

Chapter 3

Characteristics of Services

This chapter is designed to highlight the critical facts essential to understanding trade in services, especially aviation services. This brief sketch of facts will provide the reader with a background for subsequent analysis. Trade in services is a new field of study. The recent explosion of work in the area makes it impossible to incorporate every detail and aspect of trade in services. Nevertheless, the following attempts to be as comprehensive as possible, picking out important facts. A definition of services is used to introduce the characteristics identified with traded services. The underlying theme is to illustrate that trade in services may differ from trade in goods. At the very least, several of the characteristics cited are more prevalent in services than in goods. After illustrating the principle features of trade in services, the list of characteristics which prevail are placed in the context of aviation services. This underlines the point that aviation services exemplify the main characteristics of other traded services.

3.1 General Characteristics

The following paragraphs review the perspectives on services economists have taken in the past and explain why a new look at services has become necessary. Then working definitions of services and trade in services are stated in order to clarify the characteristics associated with these transactions.

3.1.1 Historical Views

Perspectives on the economic role of services have changed over time. Classical economists, including Adam Smith and Karl Marx viewed services as an unproductive activity. This view lasted for over 100 years, which explains the lack of research on services and the Non-Material Production category used in socialist national accounting systems. List and the German Historical School reexamined this perspective. By the 1930's a clearly identifiable "stages" approach developed. This perspective, most closely associated with Fisher (1939) and Clark (1951), analyzes the development process of countries by stages. In the first stage of development the agrarian (or primary) sector dominates the economy. Movement into the second stage is exemplified by the increasing importance of manufacturing (the secondary sector). It was predicted that countries would proceed towards the third stage, where services (the tertiary sector) predominate.

Subsequently, the view equating services with non-traded (or non-tradable) goods increasingly pervaded the economist's accepted wisdom. It was commonly argued that services, when tradable, were not traded because transport costs connected with services were excessive, prohibiting economical trade. These ideas allowed economists to incorporate services into the existing theories on goods by accounting for non-traded goods and/or transport costs. This fit well with the preconceptions that services had low productivity rates and that they had to be produced and consumed "on the spot".

Recent events have caused economists to rethink these views. It has been observed that services provide a substantial portion of gross national product in all countries, (generally ranging from 40 percent to two-thirds), even in developing countries. This often outstrips the contribution of the industrial sector, (UNCTAD, 1985, p. 14). These observations conflict directly with the "stages" approach. A second phenomenon causing economists to think afresh about services includes the revolutionary changes occurring in information technologies. The combination of telecommunications with computer advances increasingly permits and enhances the tradability of many services. This has happened either through the lowering of transport costs or through the provision of alternative channels to transact services. Conventional economic models dealing with services are becoming obsolete. The third motivation for this new look at services results from actions taking place in the political arena. Spurred by its private service sector's search for new markets, the United States (and eventually other OECD members) pursued diplomatic courses leading to Part II of the 1986 Uruguay Ministerial Declaration on trade in services. The United States proposal to launch trade negotiations on services within the context of the Uruguay Round has been largely responsible for the explosion of work on trade in services.

3.1.2 Defining Services

Many argue that a commonly agreed definition of services, let alone trade in services, is lacking. Often defined loosely, services frequently served as the residual category which included everything except agriculture, extractive and manufacturing activities. The view presented here is that a conceptualization of services exists. This definition distinguishes services from goods and it can be adapted to trade in services.

Hill (1977, p. 331) defines and analyzes the distinction between goods and services: "A service is a change in the condition of a person or a good belonging to some economic unit, which results from the activity of another economic unit, with the agreement of the former."

Some would argue that this theoretical distinction between goods and services confuses or misrepresents economically meaningful categories. Hill's controversial definition clearly does not represent a consensus view. The author's appeal to this definition simply allows a structured discussion of important characteristics of services. In spite of the deficiencies of any definition of services, the distinction is important for trade policy. The present study emphasizes the crucial characteristics of services rather than the debate surrounding the definition.

Service Production

There are several points implied by this definition. First, it is important to clarify some commonly held misconceptions. Based on this definition, the production of a service involves a change in a person or a good. Production differs from output. This distinction frequently causes confusion. Since the production of a service is a change in a person or a good, it is nonsense to talk about the output of a service as *non-storable* or *intangible*.[1] Confusion concerning these issues comes from the economist's false preconceptions; a result of thinking exclusively about goods for over 100 years. The change may last for an extended period of time and the good or person changed may be seen or touched. By its nature, however, a change in the condition of a person or a good (i.e. service production) is neither storable nor tangible.

Second, this definition is not inconsistent with a classification which divides services into two broad divisions: final consumer services and producers' services. Just as goods are separated in a definitional sense from capital, (goods used to produce other goods), final consumer services can be separated from producers' services, (services used to produce other services).[2] Nevertheless, distinguishing between final consumer and producers' services is not important for the purposes of this book.

---

[1] The author is grateful to Phedon Nicolaides and Harsha Singh for underlining the importance of this distinction.

[2] Significant contributions to the understanding of services have been made by stressing the importance of producers services in the economy and emphasizing the notion of "interlinkages", (Lanvin, 1988, 1989 and UNCTAD, 1985).

Service Output Measurement

The homogeneity assumption often used in economics for goods applies less readily to services. Since services involve changes in persons or goods it is difficult, and sometimes impossible, to standardize service output. It is more difficult to perceive the transport of a person from New York to London as the same output as transport from New York to Mexico City, especially for the consumer. This simple point underlines a whole host of characteristics distinguishing services from goods. While many of these features are shared with certain goods, it is argued that they are much more prevalent in services.

Service output measurements are complicated by the prevalence of quality differences, product differentiation[3] and bundling of services and goods into a single salable "product" output. As noted above, similar services do not always alter the person or the good in the same way. This problem of distinguishing quality differences immediately spills over to difficulties in measuring prices. Consumers and producers of services are not concerned only with service quality or with price; the importance of quality/price ratios preoccupy market actors.

A related issue is the ability of producers and the desire of consumers for differentiated outputs. Not only is it easy to have different quality/price ratios in services, it is actually sought by consumers and producers. Consumers and producers seek these differentiated outputs for different reasons. On one hand, consumers would like to have services which are customized and personalized to fit their particular needs. (Trade models by Lancaster (1979) and Helpman (1981) apply to this case.) An individual consumer also may prefer a variety of service quality/price combinations to fit several of his different needs. (Trade models by Dixit and Stiglitz (1977) and Krugman (1979) describe this situation.) On the other hand, producers seek output differentiation primarily to exploit some market power and to gain economies of scope, through shared inputs into joint

---

[3]Important work on this topic has been done by Orio Giarini and Jacques de Bandt, (see Bressand and Nicolaïdis (1989) for some recent examples of their work).

production processes. Output differentiation allows firms to segment the market, raising concentration and potentially reducing competition.

The exploitation of economies of scope is critical to the argument of this book. As noted in the previous chapter, economies of scope relate to cost savings associated with the joint production of different product lines. Panzar and Willig (1981) and Baumol, Panzar, and Willig (1982) carefully develop this concept within the field of industrial organization. Joint production of several different varieties for several differentiated or segmented markets permits firms to attain economies of scope. The economies of scope alledged in aviation services has general application to other services. Economies of scope are applicable for two associated reasons. First, services often are "packaged" into bundles of characteristics. Goods may be combined with services to sell to the consumer. The mixture of goods and services, as well as the differentiation of these outputs potentially provide an avenue for the exploitation of economies of scope. Second, the networking element in the production process, (via distribution, information links or personal contacts), exemplify another channel making economies of scope relevant. As UNCTAD (1988, p. 12) put it:

> Those firms which have been able to link the producer service inputs at three stages of production, i.e. 'upstream', 'onstream' and 'downstream', into a continuous 'network' or 'system' have demonstrated success in the world market, as they are able to maintain the continuous process of innovation and adaptation which the exigencies of the world market presently require.

Moreover, the nature of services reinforces the requirement that a firm maintains and builds up its reputation. The bundling and unbundling of these different varieties along with the ability to link these differentiated outputs with ancillary networks enhances the firm's competitive position.

Regulation

Perhaps more important than a theoretical definition of services, one must note that regulation of services occurs more frequently than regulation of goods. Hindley and Smith (1984, p. 377) state: "It is very striking that at the domestic level, in almost all economies, the service sector is the target of government intervention and regulation of a nature and degree which is different from the intervention to which non-service activities are subject." Regulation is one of the most important features of services that ought to be taken into account. This is another characteristic important to aviation services that contains more general application.

Despite the extensive list of regulations available to governments, one can classify regulations into a small number of categories: 1) consumer protection, 2) standards maintenance, 3) national security and prestige, 4) cultural preservation, 5) encouragement of competition, 6) ensuring sound investment, 7) protecting monetary or other domestic economic policy independence, and 8) environmental and 9) others. Obviously this does not constitute a mutually exclusive typology. However the list shows the variety of claims rationalizing regulation. Rent-seeking certainly plays a role behind many of these rationalizations. Within the "other" category one could add deliberate acts designed to discriminate against foreign competition. However, this discrimination exists to a certain extent in all other types. The problem becomes one of distinguishing between those legitimate (sometimes called "appropriate") regulations designed to protect the rights of consumers, producers, or countries and those designed simply to discriminated against foreign competition without justifiable cause. The distinction is difficult because the significance of phrases such as "appropriate regulation" and "justifiable cause" is unclear. This topic will be approached again in more detail in the policy conclusions chapter.

Countries regulate their services in a variety of ways and for several different reasons, often without regard for the impacts on trade. As Grubel (1986a, p. 23) phrased it:

> In the field of financial, insurance, transportation and similar services
> most countries have erected pervasive nets of regulation to deal with
> what have been perceived to be serious externalities arising from the
> free operation of markets. These regulations typically restrict all com-
> petition. Keeping out foreign competitors is merely a by-product. In-
> terest groups which have benefitted from this regulation have opposed,
> more or less successfully, sweeping deregulation in many of these in-
> dustries. They have done so in spite of a persuasive body of evidence
> that it would result in an increase in total welfare.

This comment points out three important elements of regulation. First, some
of the "serious externalities" could be related to the fears associated with the
exploitation of market power, which corresponds to the discussion above. A second
and more forceful argument relies upon hedonistic motivations. Important avenues
of investigation related to regulation, its causes, and manifestations follow from
public choice theory and the related rent-seeking work.[4] Third, the international
effects of regulation based on domestic concerns cannot be overlooked.

Recent trends, such as privatization and deregulation, have drawn attention to
this difficult subject. In many sectors of the economy nations have chosen to pri-
vatize or deregulate, (or at least liberalize), service sectors previously guarded by
the public sector. Air transport, (both airlines and airports), public utilities, telephone systems, trucking, rail transport, stock brokerage, etc. have all experienced
deregulation, liberalization or privatization.[5]

---

[4]Buchanan, Tollison and Tollock (1980) provide a compendium of classic articles. Kahn
(1988) is a standard reference and Spulber (1989) illustrates some recent advances.

[5]Peltzman (1989) analyzes these events and notes the relevance of the economic theory of
regulation.

3.1.3 Characteristics of Trade in Services

The exploration of a feasible definition of services highlighted three essential facts. Services are potentially prone to imperfectly competitive market structures. Concomitantly, economies of scope could play an important role in the cost structure of a service firm. Finally, the preponderance of regulation of services provides a theme that analysis must take into consideration.

Before exploring another interesting implication, it will be important to adapt the definition to *trade* in services. It suffices to add to Hill's definition that the economic unit or his good that receives or provides the change does not share the same residency with the other economic unit. This insures that the changes are international transactions and has the added advantage of relying on similar conceptualization used by the International Monetary Fund (IMF) to measure balance of payments transactions in services. It is important to note that the IMF is the main source of data on trade in services.

The IMF Definition

The working definition used by the IMF (1977) relies on differentiating residents from non-residents for the purpose of identifying international service transactions. The categories measured are relics from the views of the past. Economic activities are categorized by their outputs, which is usually convenient for trade in agricultural products and manufacturing. However, this categorization based on outputs is not consistent with Hill's definition, and therefore confuses the distinction. For example, when machine parts cross a border for assembly and then are shipped overseas as a machine the trade in parts and in machines is recorded as goods trade when this is actually trade in (assembly) services. Assuming that transborder movements of parts and machines fall under different Standard International Trade Classification (SITC) subcategories, this must be considered inter-industry trade in goods and not trade in assembly services. The problem is more complex when one considers that trade in services and goods often takes place simultaneously (e.g. leasing). Thus, at least for the foreseeable future, empirical work has to rely on data which imperfectly measures trade in services.

Simultaneity and Proximity

This definition of trade in services implies simultaneous interaction of the consumer and the producer (or their possessions). Simultaneity in time does not necessarily imply geographical proximity, as a look at the so called Sampson and Snape (1985) Box illustrates.[6] Note that the concepts of producer and receiver

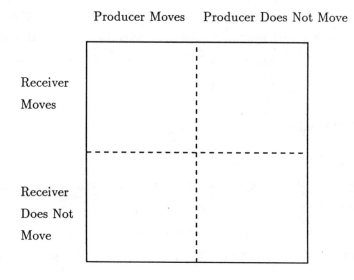

Figure 3.1: The "Sampson and Snape" Box

are expanded here to include either the person or the good owned by the economic unit. The revolution in information technologies allows many services to shift from one part of the box to another. Telecommunications has "disembodied" many ser-

---

[6]This box did not actually appear in Sampson and Snape (1985) but its construction is usually attributed to the ideas contained in that article.

vices and, as a result, neither the producer nor the receiver need move when one applies these technologies, (Bhagwati, 1984). These can be labelled long-distance services and are found in the lower right-hand corner of the box. Another type of trade in services which fits into this part of the box includes services wholly embodied in goods. Thus, the example used above concerning the assembly of machine parts belongs to this category. In all other cases the proximity of the producer and the receiver is important for the service to take place.

Modes of Transmission

The mode of international transmission of a service corresponds directly to the proximity issue. Clearly two possible modes directly derived from the definition include the movement of people and the movement of goods. The service "output" moves across international borders as embodied in the person or good changed as a result of the service. Alternatively, the movement of the person or good may be part of the service rendered. The possibility of "long-distancing" services adds two other modes of transmission: money and information, (see UNCTAD, 1988). In these cases the international transmission causing a change in the condition of the person or good results in the international movement of money or information instead of the person or the good. Just as the same services can be transacted using alternative provider/receipient proximities, modern international services can flow via any of these modes of transmission. Therefore, faced with any particular barrier to trade, economic agents desiring to undertake a service transaction can and will explore any viable alternative proximity or transmission mode evading the barrier.

International Regulation

As Grubel (1986a) observed, domestic regulation has consquences for international trade. At the same time it cannot be forgotten that international regulations perform functions similar to domestic regulations. Internationally regulated sectors include air transport, shipping, telecommunications, and intellectual property rights. All of these areas have an associated international organization: ICAO, UNCTAD, ITU, and WIPO. Some of the motivations for domestic regulation find their parallels in the international scene. The search for "appropriate" international regulation of services continues alongside the quest for proper domestic rule-making. In addition, as the liberalization trend continues domestically, similar multilateral pressure exerts itself in the European Community and in the context of the Uruguay Round of Multilateral Trade Negotiations.

3.2   Aviation Charateristics: a typical service

After exhibiting the inadequacies of previous perspectives on services, the chapter explored Hill's definition of services and adapted it to international trade. The definition provides the basis for several key concepts relevant to trade in services. Services, as changes, involve: 1) simultaneity in time, 2) elements of product differentiation including segmentation of markets, 3) potential economies of scope, and 4) pervasive regulation and trends towards deregulation, liberalization and/or privatization.

Trade in international civil aviation services has all of these characteristics and in many ways could be considered typical. As noted the nature of a service transaction often requires the simultaneous interaction of a receiver and a provider. In international aviation the service cannot be rendered unless the passenger (or the goods in the case of air freight) are physically on the aircraft. Simultaneity in time obviously occurs when passengers are transported internationally. Geographical proximity, on the other hand, is not as straight forward since the service involves the movement of people and goods. It is interesting to note that the Sampson and Snape (1985) proximity classification awkwardly groups aviation services depending upon the carrier's traffic rights. Exports on the domestic flight requires the consumer to move to the location of the producer, placing this trade in the upper right-hand corner of the "Sampson and Snape" box. Fifth freedom flights require that the producer move to the location(s) of the consumer, (the lower left-hand corner of the box). Since the act of changing locations is the major part of the service provided, proximity is essential but who moves towards whom is irrelevant.

Aviation services also exemplify characteristics of product differentiation. The discussion of the non-homogeneous nature of services above made explicit reference to aviation. Although "an airline seat is an airline seat", quality differences contribute to differentiation. First class customers may obtain a bundle of characteristics associated with their flight between two cities. Some of these features may include seat availability on demand, more convenient flght times, better check-in and waiting lounge arrangements, better in-flight food, seating and service, and more prompt deplaning and baggage handling. Airlines also attempt to appeal to the first class passengers' feeling of importance. Various gradations of these quality differences are used by carriers to differentiate the quality of seats by class and help justify price differences. Assessment of quality/price ratios in aviation presents a difficult and interesting task but one which is not attempted here.

An associated issue is the differentiation of airplane seats by destination. It has been observed that regulation aids the segmentation of markets internationally through the lattice of bilateral air service agreements. Passengers flying to a variety of cities from any given airport purchase a different, or at least differentiated air service. Airline companies attempt to differentiate their services by offering alternative routes for passengers' origin and ultimate destination pairings. These alternatives are limited by the bilateral agreements. Markets are segmented via regulation simply because the airlines allowed to fly on a particular route are restricted. Segmentation increases the level of concentration, frequently to one or two airlines, and consequently drastically reduces the amount of competition on the route. Many service transactions take place in segmented markets created through customization, regulation or both. In the case of international civil aviation services both are present but regulation clearly dominates.

Market segmentation through regulation influences the network economies achieved by an airline. The economies of scope concept rests on the ability of a producer to jointly produce different product lines using shared inputs to gain cost savings. In aviation the hubbing-and-spoking technique allows different product lines, defined via market segmentation, to be combined in a manner that yields cost savings. Economies of scope in aviation may also exist in the broader aviation service package that incorporates all the quality outputs necessary to provide passenger transport. A more holistic view could see potential economies of scope in the production of aviation services which combine passenger transport with air freight and mail delivery. Alternatively, scope economies may play a role in the provision of services that use aviation transport as an input (e.g. tourism, international consultancies, etc.). Broader views extend beyond the scope of the present work but illustrate the point that since aviation services exhibit economies of scope, they are typical of many other service transactions.

Regulation of domestic aviation compounds the restrictions imposed by international agreements including bialterals. Appropriate regulations, such as those agreed at the Chicago Convention and supervised by ICAO cover more technical aspects of safety and maintanence. Some domestic regulations pertain to these areas. Domestic and international aviation regulations have economic impacts, although sometimes these are inadvertent. As noted in Chapter 2, international regulation of capacity, fares, routes, etc. substantially affect the provision of aviation services. Domestic regulations frequently influence similar variables. Government ownership alone may reduce or eliminate an airline's profit-seeking motivation, and thereby its managment efficiency. Routes are sometimes designated, prices restricted by ceilings and floors, and capacity allocated or reserved. The nexus between domestic and international regulations are often overlooked, but will be treated in the chapter outlining policy conclusions.

Regulation has been extensive yet changing over time. The U.S. experience with deregulation of primarily economic aspects of domestic aviation services has come concomitantly·with shifts to the regulation contained in some bilateral accords. More liberal bilaterals between the U.S. and some European countries has incited some limited liberalization reactions between European nations. Pressure from the increasingly successful Asian carriers will promote the trend. However, vested interests, particularly from less competitive airlines, will seek to slow it down. At the same time liberalization of domestic markets is receiving greater attention. After the U.S. moves, the U.K. and other members of the European Community must take steps as individual nations and collectively to really create one market in aviation services. Similarly Australia and New Zealand are taking a fresh look at domestic regulations in aviation services. In November 1990 the formal duopolistic policy will end in Australia, although many impediments to competition and greater efficiency will remain. New Zealand has already privatized Air New Zealand and made the domestic market more competitive. Consideration of privatization of flag carriers, or at least more private sector involvement and promotion of profit incentives in those airlines may be a feature of the emerging agenda.

3.3   Why International Aviation Services?

Trade in aviation services (i.e. the transport of people across international boundaries) shares many of the characteristics outlined including simultaneity, aspects of product differentiation, and regulation. In the field of deregulation, aviation is the classic example. International aviation services comprise a highly visible service familiar to many people. Thus, it provides an interesting and important illustration of a service provided and consumed but not commonly considered a traded economic activity.

The microeconomist's job has become much more difficult in recent years with the advent of increased interlinkages resulting from the advantages obtained from technological innovation in services. Services are frequently referred to as the glue which holds the economy together. The infrastructural role played by traditional services, (transportation, education, health, national security), has been supplemented and in many cases supplanted by the new services in communications and computers (informatics and telematics) which have drastically altered the global economic environment. It has become unrealistic to think about individual activities and their contributions to employment, productivity, and growth. The new "glue" shifts the economist's focus to the interconnected sectors which combine production activities with service provisions to generate a more broadly defined end-product. The concentration on scheduled international aviation services is merely a slice in the air transportation industry which runs from the design and construction of airplanes and airports, to their finance, to check-in/on-board services, to air traffic control, to baggage handling, to computerized reservations, to tourist packages, to travel agencies, to hotel and restaurant services, to car and limousine rentals and other supplementary services. On the whole, however, focus on international scheduled aviation services is a good first step towards a better understanding of trade in services.

Chapter 4

Trade in Services

4.1 A Fresh Look

Much of the motivation for the fresh look at services trade comes from the Group of Negotiations on Services (GNS) being conducted in the context of the Uruguay Round of Multilateral Trade Negotiations. The realization that services, which generate substantial employment, gross domestic product, and a surprising amount of world trade, has encouraged the establishment of several study centers devoted to services. For example, the Services World Forum meets annually in Geneva to compare notes on the discoveries made concerning the global service economy (Bressand and Nicolaïdis, 1989). Other Geneva based organizations dealing with services topics include the Research Programme on the Service Economy (PROGRES), The Geneva Association, and the Applied Service Economic Centre. The Fishman-Davidson Center for the Study of the Service Sector was established in 1982 at the Wharton School and has made significant contributions already (e.g. Inman, 1985). National coalitions of service industries have organized in the United States, United Kingdom, Australia, Japan, Sweden, Argentina, New Zealand and Hong Kong. In addition to coordinating the interests of service industries domestically, the coalitions have held their sixth annual international conference in 1990 to discuss topics of mutual interest at an international level.

Considerable resources are now being used to analyze trade in services. The following pages assemble some of the interesting results and describe the continuing debates among experts. One of the most important confusions involves the debate regarding the applicability of comparative advantage and the usefulness of the Heckscher-Ohlin paradigm of trade based on relative factor endowments. Another avenue of thought leads to analysis of the role of economies of scope and scale in services trade, drawing on the so called new international trade theory of imperfect competition. Those debates often touch on issues of measurement, service quality and prices, and the linkages between goods and services. In addition, the identification of barriers to trade in services is essential to make sense of the impending moves towards liberalization in the GNS. Issues concerning developing countries and the role of services in the development process logically preceed a preliminary assessment of the trade in services negotiations at the end of this chapter.

Bringing trade in services into the negotiating limelight was followed by a plethora of academic scrambling to gain a better understanding of services trade. The sequence of events is an unusual feature of the negotiations, (Nicolaïdis, 1989). As a result of this rush for knowledge several misleading conclusions can be found in early work. Due to data limitations, heavy reliance on the Fisher-Clark stages hypothesis (described in the previous chapter) and oversimplification, authors drew policy conclusions that are not well supported by facts.

Observers of the U.S. economy noted that service sector employment was expanding rapidly and alledged that service labor productivity lagged behind manufacturing labor productivity. The conclusion intimated was that the U.S., as an emerging service economy, was going to suffer decling productivity. Thus only a conscious government industrial policy favoring manufacturing and obstructing service activities would ensure growth in the U.S. economy. Whether or not labor productivity in services is lower than in manufacturing is subject to empirical debate. However it is clear that this generalization does not hold over all disaggregated service sectors. More importantly, this hypothesis overlooks three critical facts. First, goods and services are not always distinct. The line between these two outputs blurs as one considers: 1) "in house" versus "out of house" production, that is intrafirm services, 2) the bundling of goods and services together creating joint sales, 3) the mode of delivery of certain services via goods (i.e. disquettes), and 4) alternative packaging of outputs as a good or a service (a letter versus a telephone message), (Stern and Hoekman, 1988, p. 272 fn. 2). The second fact overlooked is that technological advances have been particularly strong in many service sectors substantially raising labor productivity across the economy. Finally the concern ignores the fact that services provide infrastructure and substantial proportions of value added in the production of goods.

Early study of trade in services led some analysts to conjecture that a new international division of labor would result from the emerging global service economy. Again looking at the U.S. situation, the services trade account appears heavily in surplus (if factor services trade in capital is included). Many developing countries exhibit deficits on this account. The projected result was that the U.S. and similar countries would increasingly specialize in services and the developing countries would specialize in goods production. Aggregating at this level allows this broad generalization to appear to make sense. On the other hand, several developing countries have been extremely sucessful in exporting services. Indeed cheaper labor (from China or Mexico to the U.S.) is an example of developing countries services exports, but so are television program exports (e.g. from Brazil), tourism, construction, entrepot trading, and even aviation services. At the same time the U.S. imports considerable amounts of services and has had net imports of non-factor services.

One of the heated debates about trade in services is the confusion over the applicability of comparative advantage. It is interesting to juxtapose two recent statements by American economists. On one side are those who suspect that the theory of comparative advantage, which applies to goods, does not hold because services display different characteristics compared with goods. Noting that some economists have been in favor of applying the theory of comparative advantage to services, Geza Feketekuty (1989, p. 192) wrote:

> While the proponents of such views have recognized that trade in services is different in some respects from trade in goods, they argue that these differences do not lead to logical inconsistencies with the theory of comparative advantage. The theory of comparative advantage and other traditional models are not adequate, however, for analyzing all the issues that relate to trade in services, given some of the unique characteristics of such trade.

In stark contrast, Richard Cooper (1988, p. 254) stated:

> I think of comparative advantage as a very simple idea, universally valid, not subject to debate. Individuals, communities and even nations perform certain tasks with different efficiencies. Reliance on comparative advantage is the simple proposition that there is mutual gain to be had by each community concentrating on that activity which it does relatively more efficiently than do other communities. That proposition is always valid. True, there are different theories to explain the structure of comparative advantage that communities may have. Some of those theories, perhaps all of them, are wrong, and their validity can certainly be debated, but the theorem of comparative advantage as such cannot. ... at any moment in time, comparative advantage exists in services just as it does in the production of goods.

The allegation that comparative advantage does not hold for trade in services is merely a confusion between the concept of comparative advantage and the Heckscher-Ohlin paradigm of trade based on factor endowments. As the standard paradigm it is understandable that individuals confuse these ideas. However, because of the special characteristics of services and their trade, it is vital that the distinction be maintained. There are three ways to approach the principle of comparative advantage. Trade between two countries based on comparative advantage can rely on relative output prices, relative costs or net factor flows. There are obvious measurement problems when applying comparative advantage to services. Using relative prices may not lead to sensible trade predictions because prices may not reflect regulatory conditions and difficult to perceive quality differences. Similarly, comparative costs may be hard to obtain, and harder to associate with a given output (service provision) due to shared inputs across a bundle of goods and services. Net factor flows provide a useful theoretical description but may not be measurable. Some factor inputs may not have to traverse the national border during the production or trading process. The cause for differences in these measures of comparative advantage can be due *inter alia* to differences in factor endowments (i.e. the Heckscher-Ohlin framework), technological differences, differences in consumer tastes, the presence of economies or imperfect competition. The discussion below will underline the distinction between comparative advantage and the Heckscher-Ohlin trade predictions. Before launching the analysis of related work it is worth reviewing the special characteristics of trade in services discussed above.

4.2   The Theory of Trade in Services

Alteration of Hill's definition of services to fit international service transactions underlined three central points. International trade in services involves simultaneity but not necessarily proximity in the production of the service. Further, even similar international service transactions can be observed via several different modes of transmission. Most importantly, the pervasive role of regulation requires any model of trade in services to analyze explicitly the role of the regulatory environment and any possible alterations in the regulatory regime. Ultimately the following compares some trade models against the characteristics derived from the definitions of services and trade in services described previously.

The theory of trade in services is in its infancy. The following subsection illuminates some of the misgivings of the standard factor endowments paradigm. The second subsection discusses the few theoretical papers that have been written on the subject. Cognizant of the potential problems of the standard paradigm, the third subsection contains an analysis based on the characteristics identified in the preceeding chapter.

4.2.1   Problems with the Standard Paradigm

Despite the rapid expansion of written work on services, little trade theory on services has been written. This is understandable. For centuries services were thought of as unimportant, unproductive, a residual, or non-tradable. Recent focus on the significant contribution of domestic services production has shown it is not unusual to have this sector account for more than half of national income. Concomitantly it is observed that this sector contributes approximately 20 percent to total trade.

Up to the present, definitional and conceptual issues on services have preoccupied the attention of economists. The new round of Multilateral Trade Negotiations (the Uruguay Round) has pointed special attention to the area; yet progress on conceptualization has been a slow learning process. It is difficult to model trade in services when one is unclear as to what constitutes a service, how services are traded, and what characteristics are particular to services or traded services. This lack of theoretical modeling is compounded by the school of thought that services can already be easily handled by the existing theory of trade in goods, (see Krommenacker, 1984, p. 35).

At the same time several authors have noted that the unique features of services may render the traditional paradigm, Heckscher-Ohlin, unsatisfactory. Hill underlines the importance of the co-production of services. Both the producer and the consumer bring something to the transaction. Hill (1977, p. 319) notes that:

> In contrast to the producer of goods, the producer of services does not purchase or acquire all the inputs into his production process. The principal 'input', namely the good being serviced, continues to be owned by the consumer of the service.

The failings of the Heckscher-Ohlin framework may apply both to positive and normative results. The necessity of physical proximity for several kinds of services cause Sampson and Snape (1985) to conjecture that the traditional version of the Heckscher-Ohlin theorem insufficiently models trade. Particularly, the assumption that factors of production are immobile between countries needs to be dropped. In their words:

> As soon as trade is introduced that requires the physical proximity of the receiver of a service and the factor supplying it and the possibility of factors or receivers moving, the standard reference point breaks down. No longer are the factor endowments and receivers which are resident in a country a binding constraint. In such circumstances a new reference point to specify 'efficient trade' has to be defined. Complete freedom of movement of factors (and of receivers) appears to be the obvious candidate.(p. 178).

Moreover, for these kinds of services, preventing the relocation of factors of production provides impediments to trade. Sampson and Snape (1985, p. 179) observe:

> Restricting the movements of factors (or of receivers of services) will inhibit (i) the international movement of services (ii) the equalization

of the prices of these services internationally and (iii) the tendency to narrow the international differences in the prices of factors of production. Barriers to the movement of factors or receivers will thus provide protection to some factors of production, even if there are no barriers to trade in goods or 'separated' services.

These observations place doubt on the applicability of the standard theory of trade.

There may be more serious problems with the application of models in the standard tradition. Again Hill raises the question whether the exchange of services occurs similarly to the exchange of goods.[1] This becomes clear if one reflects on the distinction between exchange of services after their production and the exchange of goods. Services embodied in goods can be exchanged only via trade in the goods themselves. However, services embodied in people cannot be exchanged. This leads Hill (1977, p. 318) to state:

> Because services cannot be transferred from one economic unit to another, models of pure exchange economics of a Walrasian type in which existing goods are traded between economic units are quite inapplicable and irrelevant to services.

Although this is an interesting and extremely controversial statement, the remainder of this book does not follow this line of thought. The quote simply illustrates the fact that some economists have serious doubts regarding the use of traditional conceptions of trade. The generation of a non-Walrasian model of services may or may not provide insights. At present, extensions of the existing work point towards more immediate advances for trade in services research. The following section describes the state of this research.

---

[1]See Hill (1987) for a more complete analysis of this issue.

4.2.2 A Selective Review

Despite the obstacles, several authors have attempted to make contributions in this field. Most of the following ideas appeared in working papers. The reader is cautioned that this necessitates a selective approach since authors may alter significant parts of their work before publication. This survey identifies the conceptual notions currently used by economists and describes the techniques and tentative conclusions reached (or maintained) in the international theory of trade. The first segment follows the theme of articles exploring the usefulness of the Heckscher-Ohlin framework and the importance of factor endowments. It is sometimes found that the results of the Heckscher-Ohlin framework, when applied to trade in services, differ sharply from the expected results of the traditional formulation. In the second segment a separate theme relies on the assumption of economies and is generally modeled using non-Heckscher-Ohlin frameworks. These models concentrate on optimizing the welfare gains from trade given the possibility of service trade. The ultimate aim is to provide the background for analyzing the work on trade in services. The subsequent subsection will look for desirable features of a theory on trade in services based on the definitions described above.

The Importance of Factor Endowments

The analysis of trade in services is littered with papers considering the movement of factors of production and trade. Before summarizing some relevant points it should be mentioned that several authors regard factor movements distinct from trade in services (see especially Arndt, 1989). Others have dwelt upon the interesting features of factor services trade. Avoiding this debate the following paragraphs look at the theoretical work on trade in factor and non-factor services.

Deardorff's controversial 1985 paper evaluates the principle of comparative advantage as it applies to services. In contrast to Hindley and Smith (1984) who summarily conjecture that comparative advantage applies and Herman and Holst

(1981) who doubt the principle's validity, Deardorff attempts a theoretical analysis of the issue. Convinced of the necessity of a piecemeal approach to examining the relevance of comparative advantage in trade in services, Deardorff chooses three hypothetical economically important characteristics of services. For the first two characteristics, (service trade as a byproduct of goods trade and service trade as factor movements), comparative advantage holds. The third characteristic, long-distance factor trade, presents several problems. In two of three cases where this characteristic is considered, a consistent definition of the principle of comparative advantage based on relative factor endowments fails to predict trade patterns. To summarize, a model containing labor-intensive service production and a long-distance factor of service production (called management) shows that the labor abundant (management poor) country will export the management-intensive good in exchange for management services (i.e. importing the labor-intensive services). Although this contradicts the Heckscher-Ohlin theorem, this is still consistent with comparative costs. The management rich country exports pure management for the management-intensive good, which mixes some labor with management. A Ricardian version of trade with Hicks-neutral technological differences does not yield results consistent with comparative advantage based on relative factor endowments. As Jones remarks, (in comments on an earlier version of the paper), this model is consistent with comparative costs when factor prices are adjusted for quality differences. This work substantiates the distinction between comparative advantage and the Heckscher-Ohlin formulation of that theory discussed above.

Melvin (1987b) critiques the Deardorff paper because it fails "to carefully distinguish between trade in services and domestic production that uses an imported service as an input." However, Melvin agrees with the result that trade in services can conflict with Heckscher-Ohlin predictions while following the basic precepts of comparative costs. Melvin's lucid exposition of several propositions derives from a standard (two countries, two factors, two goods) model adapted for trade in factor services. The difference lies with the assumption that only one good can be traded for one factor of production. The factor of production temporarily moves, produces, and returns. These factor services are exchanged for the tradable good. One of the most important conclusions of the paper is "... in some circumstances the law of comparative advantage, at least as usually defined, need not apply to service trade." (Melvin, 1987b, p. 4). In a case where the capital-intensive good is tradable and capital is the mobile factor, the capital-rich country trades significant amounts of capital services in exchange for imports of the capital-intensive good. This trade allows the optimal allocation of world resources. However, by providing capital services in the labor abundant country, the effective global endowment position of the countries shifts. Melvin's second proposition states:

> If the tradable commodity uses the mobile factor service intensively,
> the efficient world output is possible, but the trade pattern will not be
> as predicted by the Heckscher-Ohlin theorem. (1987b, p. 16).

In the illustration the capital abundant country *imports* the capital-intensive good. As Melvin correctly points out this is another possible explanation of the Leontief Paradox. This author would add that the possibility of shifting the effective endowment point through trade in factor services enlarges the possibilities for factor price equalization, even in cases where the initial endowments and technologies would normally prevent this from occurring. Another point worth emphasizing is that a tariff on either good will always result in the same magnification effect. In other words, regardless of whether a tariff is placed on the capital-intensive or labor-intensive good, the immobile factor will gain, the mobile factor will loose and the relative price of the commodity intensive in the use of the immobile factor will rise. This is in striking contrast with the traditional formulation, where the tariff raises the relative price of the protected commodity.

Gulati and Sebastião (1986) also focus on a proximity characteristic of service production. Producers must relocate some factor to the consumers in order to provide the service. Thus the provision of a service export necessitates an additional cost when compared with domestic production. The authors analyze this situation in a two good, one service, two factor, two country model. All factor earnings abroad are assumed to remain abroad; there are no remittances, since earnings are totally reinvested. The model is a three outputs, two factors case with transport cost relevant only for one of the three "goods". Trade in the service will occur if factor relocation is permitted and if the trade is consistent with the Heckscher-Ohlin theorem. This trade can continue until the service price differential is reduced to the cost of factor relocation. However, given certain endowments and factor intensities, trade in goods may reduce this price differential sufficiently to prevent trade in the service. This implies that the service must have an extreme capital-labor ratio compared to goods for service trade to occur. The specificity and extreme nature of the assumptions prevents the model from having much practical value.

The necessity to incorporate quality, which is another point following Deardorff's article, is explored by Djajić and Kierzkowski (1986). They also use a Heckscher-Ohlin style model. The key to the model is that one of the goods is a durable, which can be produced at various different levels of quality and which requires servicing to maximize the flow of consumption. Logically the necessary amount of servicing relates inversely to the level of quality; high quality durables use less servicing over their lifetime. Services are assumed to be required only for the durable good and are produced solely with labor. The model demonstrates that, when goods trade occurs and services are not tradable, autarky prices (uncorrected for quality differences) may not reveal comparative advantage. Despite the fact that the relatively capital rich country has a comparative advantage in producing the relatively capital-intensive durable good, the durable *may* have a higher price and quality in that country; quality correlates positively with the wage-rental ratio and implies a higher price. Opening the system to trade in services can affect both the direction and the volume of trade in goods. The intuition behind this finding relies on the possibility that the relatively capital-intensive durable, when tied through a highly labor-intensive servicing contract, may exhibit a relatively labor-intensive joint production. The authors explicitly state that their model handles only one specific type of service and that other frameworks will be needed to deal with other types of services. Although some of these will call upon models identical to those used for trade in goods, others can illustrate the characteristics that differentiate services from goods.

Similar issues to the ones above are explored in a non-Heckscher-Ohlin setting by Jones and Ruane (1988), who apply a specific-factor model to illustrate the importance of technological and factor endowment differences as they affect the gains from trade. They dichotomize trade in services as either trade in service factors or trade in service products. In this model the specific service factors are mobile between countries and labor is immobile. The main reasons for trade, (technology and the endowment of skilled service factors), differ at home and abroad. Wages are given by global conditions; some factor price equalization is assumed. The supply of services is determined by local technology and the specific service factor endowment, while demand reflects local tastes and income. Ignoring income effects, the authors show that trade in the service product or the specific service factor involves gains from trade but the relative gains depend upon the countries' relative service factor endowment and relative technological comparative advantage. The maximum gains from trade through complete specialization are insured only if trade in products and factors occurs. Otherwise either service product prices or specific factor returns will equalize across countries, while the other differential expands. Finally the distributional effects of the alternative trade flows (in products or in factors) differ. If the price of the service rises, all real returns to factors other than the specific service factor fall, since other prices and nominal returns remain constant.

Theory Using Economies

Turning to the increasing returns to scale theme, Jones and Kierzkowski (1988) attempt to analyze the functions of services by separating "production blocks" from "service links". They fit their descriptive model into the literature using increasing returns to scale in the production of both blocks and links, (high fixed costs and constant marginal costs). As production becomes more sophisticated ("fragmented") more links between blocks become necessary, which by assumption yields a descending staircase of marginal costs as productivity expands. This disjoint marginal cost function allows output decisions to take discreet jumps when combined with a smooth downward sloping marginal revenue function. The authors argue that modern innovation in sectors such as transport, telecommunications and finance (service links) has accelerated and internationalized the fragmentation process. "The possibility of service linking production blocks between countries introduces gains from trade associated with the doctrine of comparative advantage." (p. 16). Part of production may occur at home and part abroad, due to the provision of service links. Services may or may not be traded but they can encourage international trade.[2]

Markusen's (1986b) discussion of on producers' services uses a Cobb-Douglas production function for the service sector and a Constant-Elasticity-of-Substitution (CES) function for the production of skilled services labor. As a result there are constant returns to scale of production to firms and to any particular specialized service and increasing returns to scale to the industry and the total number of services provided. Markusen shows that the competitive equilibrium with positive service sector output is not Pareto optimal, since it does not account for scale effects. The possibility of multiple equilibria allows the author to demonstrate that a late entrant into the increasing returns to scale service sector may be prevented

---

[2]An anonymous referee argues that transferring production blocks can cause investment flows to substitute for trade flows. Under these circumstances one could argue that the required service links mean more trade in services, but not necessarily an increase in total trade.

from providing the service and will be forced to suffer lower welfare perpetually. Similarly a small country suffers lower welfare than its larger trading partner. In fact, contraction of the increasing returns to scale production in the small country due to trade may cause a welfare loss in the smaller country. This implies that subsidies should be used to maximize welfare. Given his various assumptions, Markusen argues that a production subsidy is a first-best policy for a country, while an education subsidy to enhance skills involves a net welfare loss. Another form of optimal subsidy is the provision of public inputs by the government at no charge to the firm.

Kiezkowski (1987b) develops a simple model of strategic oligopoly to illustrate the international effects of domestic deregulation. The model incorporates both economies of scale and economies of scope in the firms' cost functions. Using a Cournot duopoly and separating the international market from the domestic market, Kierzkowski illustrates the basic point that domestic deregulation provides firms exploiting these economies with an enhanced position to compete internationally. A larger domestic market freed from regulatory practices allows greater economies and thus a competitive edge in the international market place. A simulation exercise shows these results numerically. Many of these elements will be drawn upon in later chapters.

In a separate paper, Markusen (1986a) concentrates again on producers' services, noting that these services require labor embodied with high skill levels. To obtain these skills high fixed costs must be incurred, but low marginal costs prevail in the actual provision of the service. It is argued that these cost characteristics distinguish services from standard Heckscher-Ohlin trade. This leads to increased specialization and division of labor which is limited only by the extent of the market. Borrowing from the monopolistic competition literature, Markusen places these producers' services into a CES production function for one of the goods (or services) in the model. Four conclusions result from this style of analysis. First, even identically endowed economies gain from trade. Second, a small country will gain more from trade than its larger partner, since access to greater variety of the skilled labor input enhances the final output in the sector where the input is used. This contrasts with other increasing returns to scale models (i.e. Markusen, 1986b and Kierzkowski, 1987b), where smaller countries are at a disadvantage because they cannot exploit the relevant scale economies before trading. Third, trade only in goods cannot ensure a Pareto efficient pattern of production, since some specialization is prevented. Trade in services maximizes this specialization and guarantees an optimal outcome. Fourth, a tariff does not necessarily improve national welfare, even for a monopoly power. Again, a tariff reduces the global specialization potential and diminishes the effectiveness of the optimal tariff.

4.2.3 Analysis

The work based on the factor proportions rationale for trade generally substantiates the apprehensions identified. The Heckscher-Ohlin theorem does not provide a universal key to predicting trade patterns in services, as demonstrated by Deardorff (1985), Melvin (1987b) and Djajić and Kierzkowski (1986).

In general, papers in the factor proportions tradition emphasize the role of proximity as in Deardorff (1985), Melvin (1987b) and Gulati and Sebastiõ (1986). This characteristic was shown to hold often but not systematically, rendering these models specific to those kinds of services. Only one of the papers in the Heckscher-Ohlin tradition explored the important features of quality differences and of joint production of goods and servicing, (Djajić and Kierzkowski, 1986). However, this model appears specific to an even narrower class of services.

On the other hand, there exists an entire subdivision of papers that incorporates economies in some form. These models generally take the market structure into account, e.g. Markusen (1986a, 1986b) and Kierzkowski (1987b). Only two papers attempt to broach the subject of the regulatory environment. Markusen (1986b) discusses the welfare maximizing use of subsidies and Kierzkowski (1987b) directly attacks the effects of deregulation in the domestic market.

A model which incorporates elements of imperfect competition and some form of economies with simultaneity and analysis of the role of international regulation as well as changes in the regulatory environment would make an important contribution. As a preliminary step, an indepth study of a particular service sector exemplifying many of these features may prove useful. This is the rationale for the development of such a model for trade in international aviation services.

4.3   Empiricism in Trade in Services

Having reviewed the theory on trade in services, it is appropriate to look at the results of empirical studies in the field. The paucity of data has severely restricted the number of attempts to test trade hypotheses against observations concerning services. This section surveys three papers addressing trade in all services and one paper which looks at trade in transportation services. The brief summary of empirical work on trade in services is sufficient to reiterate the doubt regarding the Heckscher-Ohlin theorem, the potential usefulness of imperfectly competitive models and the need to explore sectoral studies.

One of the earliest empirical studies of trade in services, Dick and Dicke (1979) analyzed the knowledge intensive nature of trade. Using 1973 Organization for Economic Cooperation and Development balance of payments data for 18 countries, the authors tested four alternative models of trade in knowledge in goods and services. The services considered knowledge-intensive included: freight and insurance on merchandise, other transportation and other private services. They tested the extended version of the Heckscher-Ohlin theorem, the stages of development (or income) hypothesis, the neo-technological hypothesis, and the endowments in natural resources hypothesis. The authors used the following explanatory variables: gross domestic product per capita, the supply of skilled labor, research and development expenditure, natural resource endowment, market size measured by population, final government expenditures, and real capital inflows. None of the models were capable of explaining knowledge trade in services. "Even when disaggregating traded knowledge intensive services, no result was in accordance with expectations." (p. 346). On the other hand, a knowledge intensive goods model including raw materials endowments, relatively large amounts of highly skilled labor, and research and development expenditures as variables adequately explained trade patterns. The authors provided four rationalizations for the poor results concerning services. Relatively pervasive trade barriers in services could distort the results expected from standard theoretical versions of international trade. Two others are violations of these standard theories: the lack of identical production functions across countries and possible factor intensity reversals (see for example Dixit and Norman, 1980, p. 52). Complementarities between goods and services constitutes a fourth rationalization. Services trade results from goods trade, sometimes. If goods trade is capital-intensive and services are necessary, then *service* trade can violate the Heckscher-Ohlin theorem. However, overall trade need not violate the Heckscher-Ohlin theorem. The factor content version of trade will hold in either case.

In their 1980 paper for the World Bank, Sapir and Lutz use International Monetary Fund (IMF) balance of payments cross-section data for 1975 from up to 44 countries. Testing credits and debits separately for shipping, other transportation, travel, and other private services, the empirical results generally performed as expected. Sapir and Lutz imply that a loose interpretation of neo-factor proportions theory may apply to services.

In a follow-up study Sapir and Lutz (1981) call upon the standard and extended version of the Heckscher-Ohlin-Samuelson models, neo-technology theory, scale economy theory and market-imperfection theory to analyze the patterns of trade in non-factor services. The authors gathered 1977 IMF data on 52 countries. Tests of freight services, passenger services and three subcategories of insurance services included sample sizes ranging from 13 to 32 countries. The authors conclude:

> On one hand, performance in transportation services (freight and pas-
> senger services) appears to be related to capital abundance. For insur-
> ance services, performance seems, on the other hand, to hinge upon
> the availability of human capital. Location and economies of scale
> are also important in certain instances. These findings indicate that
> economies that are abundant in physical and human capital have a
> comparative advantage in services.

Sapir and Lutz mention in a footnote to this statement that human capital also
appears as the principle determinant of trade in other private services, although
they were reticent to include empirical findings for such a heterogeneous category. In addition, they argue that the results of the study are consistent with
the stages approach to comparative advantage developed by Balassa (1977). The
next chapter includes a more detailed analysis of the passenger services results,
since passenger services credits proxy for aviation services exports.

In a sectoral study on transportation services Kierzkowski (1986) tests an
oligopolistic model stylistically similar to Brander's (1981). Using quarterly data
for nine countries, the aggregation of exports of shipping plus other transportation
served as the dependent variable. Shipping implicitly dominates the formulation
of the theory and, even more so, the formulation of the empirical test. Explanatory
variables included merchandise exports, the world price of oil, wage rates of the
exporting country, and the exchange rate. A similar equation for transportation
imports was run replacing merchandise exports with merchandise imports. The
overall empirical results appear good in both tests. This led Kierzkowski (1986, p.
29) to conclude: "Broadly speaking, our preliminary empirical work suggests that
the framework of imperfect competition proposed in this paper is indeed suitable
for modeling transportation services."

These studies imply that further careful empirical work remains. Statisticians currently working to correct for the lack and poor quality of data will make the trade economist's job easier. In the meantime, creative approaches to the problem must be explored.

The theory of international trade in services contains two themes. The positive economic theme addresses the applicability of the Heckscher-Ohlin theorem. Although leading academics have not reached a consensus yet, there are doubts that the pattern of trade should follow solely from factor endowments. One must hasten to add that this does nothing to invalidate the law of comparative costs. Clearly comparative advantage holds for trade in services as it holds for trade in goods; however the basis for comparative advantage may differ. A second theme is the incorporation of economies, (usually increasing returns to scale), requiring imperfectly competitive trade models. Generally concentrating on welfare issues these models often demonstrated that trade only in goods is not welfare maximizing. Pareto optimal solutions frequently require trade in services and sometimes market intervention such as subsidization. As the papers by Markusen underline, uncertainty surrounds the welfare effects on small countries in these models. The empirical work generally supports the idea that standard economic theory may mislead service trade pattern predictions. Imperfectly competitive models may be on the right track.

4.4 Barriers to Trade in Services

As noted in Chapter 2, there are a variety of motivations for regulating domestic activities, most of which ignore their implications for international trade. Quality controls, price restrictions and entry barriers are among the regulatory options that have direct economic impacts. However, security issues, national prestige measures, environmental concerns also affect the economic circumstances of transactions. International transactions in services are influenced by domestic as well as international regulatory systems. Once again the focus on trade in services caused by the Uruguay Round has led to debate about the kinds of regulations subject to negotiation.

The mode of transmission of an international transaction varies. Money, goods, people and information cross borders singly or in combinations for the transaction to take place. Unlike trade in goods alone, barriers to trade in services usually do not take the form of customs duties assessed at national boundaries. Domestic regulation, discrimination against foreign entities and subsidization all limit or distort trade in services. The economics of non-tariff barriers to trade may require economists to rethink their standard ideas concerning the relative merits and demerits among alternative interventions. With goods trade economists generally set a preference ordering for tariffs, then quotas and then subsidies. Taxes and subsidies are thought of as expensive administrative techniques and quotas are not transparent. Besides, a functioning system within the General Agreement on Tariffs and Trade (GATT) allows transparent stand-still and roll-back of tariffs under the most-favored-nation rule. Services trade does not conform to these conditions. Most barriers to trade in services block the flow of capital, labor, information or goods, but these barriers do not necessarily occur at the border. Exchange controls, visa requirements, limited access to networks and standards regulations are among the obstacles to free flows of services.

It may be impossible and perhaps undesirable to try to quantify and transfer the equivalents of non-tariff barriers to services trade into tariffs. Although this suggestion would allow the negotiations to follow liberalization methods used for goods trade, the regulatory issues mentioned above prevent serious consideration of this idea. Thus, it will be important for future work on trade in services to attack the problem of liberalization given the prevalent form of trade barriers. Subsequent chapters attempt to incorporate various elements which need to be treated, including the role of barriers to market entry and subsidization. The concluding chapter evaluates the policy implications of the findings.

4.5   Service and Development

Ministers launching the Uruguay Round stressed the importance of development as an objective for the services negotiations. In the early stages analysts questioned the role developing countries have to play in negotiations on services trade. Others attempted to persuade the developing countries that it was in their interest to participate in these talks. Although a final verdict has not been reached, it is clear that different countries have different interests in the negotiations on services. As noted above a division of labor which efficiently allocates goods production to developing countries and services production to more economically advanced nations does not follow the facts. The negotiating table will be surrounded by a plethora of overlapping interest groups, depending upon the sector or regulatory issue under discussion.

The positive role of services in the development process is unquestionable. Basic infrastructural services have always been at the heart of successful development. Transport, health, education, communications and financial institutions provide the grease that makes the wheels of agriculture, extractive sectors, and industry move smoothly. Services are becoming more than just the glue that holds the economy together. Technological advances in computers and telecommunications have seeped through the entire fabric of the global service economy. Access to information and networks has become a critical element of economic development. Unbundling and repackaging goods and services to form innovative production processes, distribution systems and consumer oriented outputs make these new services essential.

The development and trade nexus appears as a constant theme. The transitions taking place in the global service economy provide risk and opportunities previously unknown. The previous pages underlined the scepticism among economists of the validity of the simple Heckscher-Ohlin theorem based on factor endowments. Analysts of trade in services are exploring the changes necessitated by characteristics of networks and resulting economies (of scope and scale), quality characteristics, and regulation. Some observers consider information as a factor of production (Lanvin, 1989). What this implies for development is interesting. Exploiting comparative advantage does not necessarily mean simply relying on factor endowments. It implies new possibilities of comparative advantage which encompass factor endowments, information and networking capabilities. Regulatory influences as barriers to trade in services and goods will distort optimal exploitation of comparative advantage and retard development acheivable through trade. Again extention of this discussion takes place in the concluding chapter.

4.6   Some GNS Issues

The Uruguay Round Group of Negotiations on Services will not limit itself to discussion of liberalization and development issues as regards trade in services. Principles of trade in services and sectoral delimitations also are included. Although more extensive discussion of these matters follow in the concluding chapter, it is appropriate at this juncture to ennumerate some of the priciples as background to the pages that follow. It has effectively been argued (Feketekuty, 1989) that despite characteristics that differentiate goods from services trade, the principles of the GATT articles of agreement should apply to all trade. Specific forms, rule and procedures following these principles may need to be adapted to conform with the various characteristics particular to services.

The main prinicples include unconditional most favored nation (MFN) treatment, national treatment, transparency, and progressive liberalization. This is not an exhaustive list. Briefly, unconditional MFN means that all parties to the agreement automatically benefit from any move towards liberalized trade made between any two parties. Although this principle is abrogated frequently within the GATT (through free trade areas or special and diffential treatment for developing countries), the lesson learned in the 1930's with destructive bilateral trade is worth remembering. In addition, this makes the liberalization process potentially faster and more politically palatable. National treatment allows producers operating in foreign markets to receive no less favorable treatment than domestic producers. Nationalized service providers and special regulatory conditions point to the difficulty many nations would have in applying this principle to services. On the other hand, it would force regulators primarily concerned with domestic considerations to explicitly account for the trade implications of their rules. Transparency allows easy identification of trade barriers and therefore simplifies liberalization processes. Making the non-tariff barriers to trade in services transparent presents a formidable task. The application of an inventory approach to grandfathering and eventually rolling back services trade barriers receives further attention in the concluding chapter, where other elements of the GNS talks are discussed.

Chapter 5

Trade in Aviation Services

Many problems slow the progress of research on trade in services. To add to the difficult conceptualization and characterization process and to the correspondingly difficult task of modeling these features as they relate to trade, the lack of good data has hindered the analysis of trade in services. Much work has proceeded in the past few years, however it will take several more years, at least, to generate the data requirements for thorough empirical study (especially bilateral data). Preliminary work, such as those cited in the previous chapter, has stretched the balance of payments statistics quite far. Although more useful work can be done, especially with the longer time series now available, it appears that a sectoral approach to these isuues also may bear fruit. This seems doubly attractive since the work of the GNS increasingly focuses attention on individual service sectors. Several important sectors, particularly those with long established international organizations designed to deal with sector specific areas, have a hidden supply of relevant data. The organizations assigned to specific sectors have rarely focused directly on trade issues until quite recently and they certainly have not approached this topic within the broader context of trade in services. (UNCTAD's work on shipping and insurance, and the UNCTC's work on transborder data flows are the exceptions.)

Moreover, a sector specific approach avoids the difficulties of developing a general model to deal with such a heterogeneous category of economic activities. On the other hand, a trade model designed to incorporate specifics of a service sector will stress the similarities and differences with trade in other service sectors and, of course, with goods trade.

An appropriate procedure to follow is to analyze the fundamental economic factors of the service sector with a mind towards developing a useful model which implies conclusions concerning trade in that service. The present chapter contains this analysis. Development of that model constitutes step two, while empirical testing of the model, step three, should follow. After conclusion of this exercise an assessment of the lessons learned and broader implications for trade in services is possible, as step four. These steps are followed in this volume.

Little has been written on trade in aviation services. International aviation services share many of the features of other services trade including regulation and moves toward deregulation, the growing importance of networks and economies (of scope) in production. Study of this sector sheds light on other trade in services. This chapter clarifies the concept of international trade in aviation services, analyzes the possible trade theories applicable to this trade, and recapitulates the few empirical studies applying these theories. Some interesting aviation, development and trade policy issues are also raised. This will contribute to the search for an appropriate trade model.

5.1   Concepts

A residency approach to trade in aviation services is consistent with International Monetary Fund balance of payments accounting. In principle a country exports aviation services when an airline, (a resident), from that country sells its services to a passenger resident in another country. Practical measurements and corresponding overestimates and underestimates resulting from this procedure are discussed in Chapter 7.

There are several interesting observations that can be made about this definition of trade in aviation services. First, aviation services commonly involve intra-industry trade. When TAP AIR PORTUGAL, (the Portuguese flag carrier), flys from Lisbon to Geneva it is carrying Portuguese and non-Portuguese residents. Only the sale of services to non-Portuguese residents are considered exports, since sales to residents of Portugal are domestic transactions. Assume for a moment that some of these non-Portuguese are Swiss residents. SWISSAIR sales to non-Swiss residents on the Lisbon-Geneva route may be partially composed of Portuguese residents. Portugal exports aviation services to Switzerland while Switzerland exports aviation services to Portugal; this is intra-industry trade. In principle the TAP flight from Lisbon to Faro, a domestic route, may also involve exports. Sales to non-Portugese residents for this flight are equally considered exports.[1]

Two other characteristics of services obviously apply to trade in aviation services. First, aviation services involve the simultaneous interaction of the producer and the receiver, to alter the receiver's location. Passengers and airplanes must come together at the same time to change the passengers' location. Second, markets are easily separable and therefore service outputs are easily differentiated. As noted earlier, flying from New York to London is clearly differentiable from a flight between New York and Mexico City. This second feature points to the exploration of imperfectly competitive models of trade in aviation services.

Another crucially important feature that traded aviation services have in common with many other services is that they are regulated. Previous pages have described international regulation of entry, output, and prices through bilaterals in detail. Certainly these agreements provide impediments to trade in aviation

---

[1]Professor Sapir makes the astute observation that this example may not really show intra-industry trade, if the airlines are party to a pooling arrangement, (see above). To the extent that pooling occurs, intra-industry trade may vanish or, at least, diminish. As noted above, this appears primarily within the European context.

services. Domestic regulation even in "deregulated" countries also obstruct trade. National regulation often prevents foreign-ownership of an airline based in its territory. Besides these restrictions on foreign investment or establishment, cabotage traffic rights rarely are granted. Even the "deregulated" U.S. domestic market reserves these rights to U.S. residents, (see Koten, 1987). Considering the importance of hubbing-and-spoking to airline efficiency, the common occurence of a national monopoly flag carrier implicitly constructs a barrier to trade. Domestic national monopolies must carry travelers from all over the country to the international gateways available in the nation. This cuts the potential traffic that could otherwise on-line from domestic origin to domestically located international gateway to a foreign destination, (or move traffic in the opposite direction). Regulation insuring domestic monopolies diminishes the potential benefits available from hubbing-and-spoking. Providing ancillary services by a single national authority further protects a nation from trade. The bias of national computer reservations systems, airports and auxilary services for baggage, passengers and aircraft shelters the national airline against foreign competition. Finally, and not least in importance is the subsidization of the flag carrier. Direct payments, and more commonly, the ability to use public funds and run losses indefinitely distorts trade in aviation services. Foreign competiton with nationally subsidized carriers has been described graphically as entering a bleeding contest with a blood bank, (Kasper, 1987, p. 11).

Passenger transportation is the act of moving people from one location to another. Proximity of consumer and producer is not the only prerequisite to trade. Trade also requires the liberty of the consumer and producer to change location. The regulatory environment analyzed above details restrictions placed on the producer. To this must be added the immigration and currency restrictions, (visas, exchange controls, etc.) that limits passengers' mobility.

In short, many of the characteristics generally attributed to traded services apply to trade in aviation services. The concepts of simultaneity, differentiation of service output, and regulation and subsidization all apply to the international trade of aviation. The next question to answer is: to what extent, if any, have the theory and tests on trade in international aviation services incorporated these characteristics?

5.2 Theory and Empiricism

Few explicit models have been developed and tested especially for trade in aviation services. Four approaches to the theory of international trade in aviation services have recently been suggested. These include perfect competition in the guise of comparative costs, explicit use of standard Heckscher-Ohlin theory, the contestable markets approach, and oligopoly.

5.2.1 Comparative Costs

One of the few papers to discuss the international trade of aviation services, written by Findlay[2] and Forsyth (1985), draws on a number of studies by these authors. The main thrust of the paper is to recapitulate the comparative cost findings of their empirical research. Implicit behind the interpretation of their results is a perfect competition trade theory consistent with the use of comparative costs to determine the pattern of trade. Details of the theoretical foundations are not specified.

Using data on 34 airlines in 1980, they regress total kilometers performed, (TKP), stage lengths, (S), load factors, (L), a skill index, (E), and the prices of labor, (W_1), and fuel, (W_2), on total costs. TKP, W_1, and W_2 were expected to be positively correlated with total costs while the other variables were anticipated to be related negatively. The coefficients obtained these expected signs and were statistically significant. Other variables that were tried and found insignificant

---

[2]The author would like to thank Christopher Findlay for comments clarifying the points presented in the following paragraphs.

included aircraft size, a government ownership dummy, capital prices, "other" inputs, and the proportion of output which was non-scheduled.

One result which caused the authors consternation was the fact that the coefficient on TKP implied the presence of economies of scale, which as they also note, contradicts earlier findings of several analysts. An increase in TKP, according to their formulation, is generated by an increase in frequency and holds everything else constant.[3] The estimation gave the result that a ten percent increase in TKP only causes an eight and one-half percent increase in total costs. "This result may not be reliable because of biases introduced by the effects of extensive regulation in international air transport."(Findlay and Forsyth, 1985, p. 8). They remark that in a regulated environment high cost firms can survive and inefficient firms are protected. This contrasts with the implicit model of perfect competition, where high cost firms would suffer losses and be forced to reduce costs or go out of business and inefficiencies would be eliminated. Compelled by the empirical evidence running counter to economies of scale, they constrain their coefficient on TKP to unity and thereby obtain estimates consistent with other cost studies.

In an attempt to account for the inefficiency biasing the sample Findlay and Forsyth calculate a frontier cost function, the lowest cost possible when firms are producing efficiently. They use this function and sample average values to compare standard output unit costs with those unit costs of each airline. This aims at a measure of an airline's long-term potential competitiveness. Although correcting for efficiency alters the results slightly, the broad conclusions remain the same. Asian airlines from developing countries have significantly lower costs than European carriers. This substantiates similar findings from other sources, (see McGowan and Trengrove, 1986; Pryke, 1987; and Sawers, 1987). These results rely upon the heavy weight placed on differential wages and skill levels. The authors imply that cheap labor costs in developing countries give them low

---

[3]As Christopher Findlay has observed, the omission of density effects may cause the low coefficient on TKP. Therefore, concluding economies of scale from this test may be misleading.

unit costs especially as skill levels rise. However, wages will rise as skills are accumulated and eventually higher productivity will not be able to offset higher labor costs. "Competitiveness in airline services is therefore associated with a particular period in the development process,"(Findlay and Forsyth, 1985, p. 10). They go on to state that liberalization would tend to bring costs to efficient levels, implying that European airlines would be made generally less competitive.

There is a caveat to this conclusion. Using a gravity model of trade, again implicitly, the authors show the importance of location to an airline's competitive position. Many inputs of aviation services must be purchased in the region where services are provided, especially on longer routes. The natural barrier of distance, therefore, can protect European airlines from cheaper Asian competition. On the other hand, higher cost Asian airlines, such as QANTAS or JAL, are at a bigger disadvantage, since they must compete locally with low cost carriers.

The authors conclude stressing that wide cost differences due to wage, skill, and efficiency differentials point to real gains from trade. Liberalization may dampen these differentials by eliminating inefficiencies, yet important gains will remain.

Three criticisms apply to this study. First, the implicit models rely on either unlikely hypotheses or purely *ad hoc* modeling. Perfect competition implied by the comparative cost method of trade analysis means the abandonment of the bilateral system or the granting of global fifth freedom rights. These measures would be required to allow a low cost carrier, (say PAL), to drive high cost carriers, (say AER LINGUS and MEXICANA), out of business by flying in competition with them, (say Dublin to Mexico City). The gravity model, on the other hand, imports no such assumptions and generally gives good results empirically. However, it provides no formal theoretical framework and therefore yields little policy guidance.

Second, the unfortunate and misleading conclusion one could draw from this research is that countries continuing on the path of development will need to encourage their protection of the aviation sector over time. This is because the authors find that natural forces, due to wage and skill changes, lead to a rise then a decline in competitiveness. Of course the authors would disagree that their evidence supports protectionist arguments. Lobbists would tend to misuse these results to gain protection for a national airline as it loses its competitiveness when wages and skills change. However, European experience shows the demerits of airline protectionism. In the aviation sector higher prices and lower service quality have penalized the European consumer (Sawers, 1987). These losses filter through the European economies to the extent that aviation services are an input into other business activities. In Europe, where airlines recieve significant protection, the authors clearly cite the welfare benefits presumably associated with liberalization. Although protection would benefit the air transport producers, given standard welfare models it adversely affects national and global welfare.

As a final criticism, trade data are ignored. Questions of the pattern of trade were not addressed using trade data. This criticism is not so powerful if the implicit model of perfect competition is assumed to apply to potential trade patterns under a new regulatory regime. Nevertheless, the use of an imperfectly competitive model of aviation services which incorporates regulatory elements into predictions of trade patterns may apply in the context of the present environment.

5.2.2   The Heckscher-Ohlin Framework

As noted previously, Sapir and Lutz (1981) call on the economist's standard model of trade under perfect competiton, the Heckscher-Ohlin or factor proportions model.[4] They hypothesize that the transportation of passengers is a capital-intensive activity. The use of the passenger services item in International Monetary Fund balance of payments statistics involves several measurement problems, (see Chapter 7), but the category primarily covers airline services. The authors

---

[4]A useful formulation can be found in Helpman and Krugman (1985, chapter 1).

postulate that countries receiving many non-resident passengers are likely exporters of air transport services and those countries whose residents often travel abroad are likely importers. (This postulation holds only if passengers do not tend to fly on the airline that shares their residency.) The authors attempt to capture this phenomenon by using the ratio of travel credits to travel debits, which consist mainly of tourist services. Regressing this ratio and a calculated capital-labor ratio on passenger services, the authors expected positive correlation with both independent variables. The data drew on 31 observations in 1977. The sample was broken down into 22 developing and nine industrializing economies.

The authors claim that "despite several factors that are left unaccounted for, it is surprising (and reassuring) to find that our theories perform so well." (Sapir and Lutz, 1981, p. 17). Yet the reported results seem inconsistent and disconcerting. Regressions were run on the whole sample and on each of the subsamples in both linear and log-linear forms. The capital-labor ratio coefficient is only significant (at the 95 percent level) twice: once in the linear equations for the whole sample and again for the developing countries sub-sample. When the simple linearity restriction is lifted and logarithums are applied, the coefficient is not significant and even has the wrong sign for the industrializing countries sub-sample. In the equation that performs the best, (linear for the whole sample), the R-squared statistic shows only 25 percent explanation. Much is left unaccounted. The authors mention that the travel credit-debit ratio is an imperfect proxy ignoring locational differences and that protectionism distorts the results.

Two further criticisms remain. First there is no theoretical justification for grouping the data by developing and industrializing economies. Why should the Heckscher-Ohlin explanation of trade in aviation services work differently between these groups? Second, the coefficients across the equations varied widely, even on the rare occasion when these were significant. Aside from these problems it may be that the Heckscher-Ohlin model may explain the essential features of trade in services and trade in aviation services in particular. Clearly further research in this area is called for before one could put more faith in this explanation of trade in aviation services.

5.2.3 Contestability

Another trade theory applicable to aviation services is derived from the contestable markets approach. Although the theory of contestable markets has had particular sway in aviation services, (e.g. it had great influence in the deregulation of the U.S. domestic market), it has not been applied directly to trade in these services. The following paragraphs look at the theory and evidence of contestable markets in aviation services in general and at the implications and casual evidence of a trade theory based on this approach.

The Contestability Hypothesis The contestability hypothesis proffered by Baumol, Panzar and Willig (1982) in the field of the industrial organization provides a new benchmark for analyzing the efficiency of markets. Less restrictive than the assumptions required by a model of perfect competition, perfect contestability insures a welfare maximizing outcome via the threat of entry by potential competitors. Incumbent firms are constrained to price their products in a manner consistent with welfare maximization. The key to this result of perfect contestability is the ability of firms to costlessly enter and exit a market. This requires zero, (or close to zero), sunk costs, equitable access to the incumbents' technology, and the speed to act before incumbents can alter their prices. These conditions result either in optimal monopoly pricing or, in all other cases, marginal cost pricing. Given this theoretical model, concentration of firms in a particular sector of the economy should not effect efficiency.

Evidence of Contestability At the dawn of the development of the theory of the contestable markets it was suggested that aviation services in a deregulated setting would prove to be an extremely good example of perfect contestability.

The point turned out to be debatable. On one hand Bailey and Friedlaender (1982, p. 1042) stated:

> If each market is readily contested, there may be no need to fear concentration at the industry level. The airline industry offers an example. This industry has capital costs which, while substantial, are not sunk costs. The bulk of airline capital (i.e. aircraft) can be flown (recovered) from any particular market at little cost, making entry and exit easy in most city-pair markets. Such markets, even if actually served by only a single firm, have the cost attributes necessary to approximate contestability.

They go on to cite Bailey and Panzar's (1981) study which provides evidence that the potential threat of entry by trunk carriers on some local markets effectively suppressed prices. On the other hand, Shepherd (1984, p.585) argued that recourse to contestability was unnecessary: "airline competition can be explained well by established concepts of market structure and entry."

The apparent consensus on this debate does not clearly support either conjecture. However, the evidence, much of which is based on U.S. experience, points toward rejection of the perfectly contestable markets approach to aviation. The evidence in favor of perfect contestability in U.S. air transport was never terribly strong. The Bailey and Panzar (1981) work cited above noted that contestability did not apply to all markets, especially those served by trunk carriers. Graham, Kaplan and Sibley (1983) report that air fares are positively correlated with their Herfindahl index of concentration, a result which is inconsistent with perfect contestability. Moore (1986) has shown similar proof of this inconsistency. Bailey, Graham and Kaplan (1985) repeat this finding during the transition to deregulation, but maintain that some form of contestability may hold in the long-run.

Dissatisfied with the implicit tests of contestability by findings that were merely inconsistent with the contestability approach, Morrison and Winston (1986,

1987) set out to explicitly compare the theoretical predictions with empirical evidence. They rely on previous work to estimate differences between passenger welfare obtained and the optimal level of welfare. They combine this with an explicit measure of potential competition, the number of competitors serving either end point of a route without serving that route. If perfect contestability prevails in U.S. aviation their measure of welfare differences should be equal to zero on those routes that have at least one potential competitor. However, their results show that none of the routes with at least one potential competitor had a zero value for their measure of actual versus optimal welfare differences. They conclude that air transport is not perfectly contestable. In spite of this conclusion the authors find that potential entry may still affect welfare, although it does not drive markets to welfare maximization. They call this a case of imperfect contestability. It is worth noting that a minimum number of potential competitors is required before they effect welfare.

Faced with the evidence two of the original promulgators of the contestability thesis, Baumol and Willig, (1986), have written: "... some studies of the airline industry conclude that the industry is less close to the model of perfect contestability than has sometimes been suggested." The reasons for this lie with the conditions required by contestability: free entry and exit, equitable access to technology, and lack of price responses by incumbents. Many authors cite the fact that sunk costs provide a barrier to entry. For example, Lazar (1989) notes that sunk costs combined with infinite horizon repeated Bertrand games imply either zero entry or zero price reductions given entry. Beesley (1986) and Baumol and Willig (1986) argue persuasively that these costs are small, if any, and do not erect a substantial barrier. In contrast, the shortage of airport facilities and access to air traffic control services provide a barrier to entry on particular markets. The patronage built up by incumbents contributes to the difficulties of free and easy entry. Second, technological changes caused by drastic alterations of jet fuel prices, aircraft size and other qualities, and route configurations have increased demand for certain kinds of aircraft. The increased orders have bottlenecked delivery and prevented equitable access to the optimal technologies. Incumbents have adapted slowly to the changes needed to compete with new carriers who have access to cheaper labor, causing another disparity in technological availability. The third condition for perfect contestability also may have been violated. To use Baumol and Willig's (1986, p. 25) words: "Moreover, when new entry does occur established carriers do reduce their fares in response, something one would expect in a conventional oligopolistic market other than one that is perfectly contestable."

Contestability and Trade   Perfect contestability has been applied to international trade theory, although not to trade in aviation services. In Helpman and Krugman's (1985) pathbreaking book on imperfect competition they devote chapter 4 to the development of such a theory. They include a good produced with increasing returns to scale, (IRS), technology. The results include factor price equalization as long as the number of constant returns to scale goods exceed the number of factors of production. The determination of which country produces the IRS good is not derivable from the model. The authors find that the basic "Vanek chain"[5] still holds, the net flows of factor services is consistent with comparative advantage as in the standard factor proportions model. Yet factor flows are not the only reason for trade. Complete specialization will cause trade in the other goods, unless the IRS good technology is coincidentally identical to the world relative factor endowment. Finally, the authors argue that gains from trade are likely even with the production of an IRS good, a constant theme of the book. Consistent with the analysis of Graham (1923), opening of trade presumably leads to expansion in the production of the IRS good and this implies global gains from trade.

---

[5]The "Vanek chain" is a method for predicting the factor content of net trade flows for a multi-factor, multi-product world, assuming factor price equalization, (see Helpman and Krugman, 1985 and Vanek, 1968). This is done by ranking products by relative factor intensities and relating trade to the embodied flow of factors.

Application of this model to trade in aviation services is inappropriate. First, as noted earlier economies of scale in aviation have not been strongly evident. However, this does not pose a problem, since economies of scope could easily be substituted for scale. More substantial problems arise in the international context. Entry and exit presently are restricted by bilateral arrangements. Even in cases where more liberalized bilaterals have been negotiated national regulation sometimes requires entrants to publicly disclose their strategy, giving incumbents a competitive edge, (see Beesley, 1986). Moreover, governments may not allow a flag carrier to simply cancel their operations on a route for reasons of national security, prestige, or other political considerations, thereby limiting exit possibilities. The airport constraints, technological differences, (especially in labor markets), and price retaliations by incumbents leads to an *a priori* rejection of the use of this model for international trade in aviation services. This will not preclude reference to this model when discussing potential policy modifications.

5.2.4   Oligopoly

Baumol and Willig's statement quoted above does lead to reflection regarding the applicability of oligopoly to trade in aviation services. Again there is a lack of empirical evidence in this direction. A recent paper by Kierzkowski (1987b) combines several features of the industrial organization and strategic international trade theory to explore the effects of domestic deregulation. He alludes directly to hypothetical examples based on air transportation. Using a simple Cournot model of oligopoly and combining economies of scope and scale together, Kierzkowski shows that freer access to a domestic market strengthens a carrier's competitive position in international markets. Due to this strategic interaction, deregulation of the domestic market by allowing increased entry reduces the incumbent carrier's position in the international setting. A simulation exercise illustrates these results.

The framework provided presents a simple and potentially applicable model of international trade in aviation services. Certain features would have to be altered to fit the circumstances of the sector and specific, testable hypotheses remain to be extracted from such a formulation. An important caveat concerning the results must be highlighted. Deregulation in the U.S. has been shown to increase densities by changing airline's networks. To the extent that this is the result of the deregulation the results of Kierzkowski's paper are reversed. Deregulation and the concomitant increase in economies of scope, working through the strategic link, could strengthen not weaken the incumbents international competitive position.

Review of the theory and evidence on trade in international aviation services reveals that perfect competition has some serious handicaps. The theory has difficulty dealing with the peculiarities of the highly regulated market. The Sapir and Lutz (1981) evidence, although consistent with the predictions of the theory, apparently lacks powerful description and is inconclusive. The appeal of perfect contestability to aviation services has been shown to be weak even in the context of the deregulated U.S. market. Transfer of the theoretical foundations to international trade is possible, but application to trade in international aviation services is dubious. Simple oligopolistic market structures may lead to more fruitful results; adaptation to the circumstances in international aviation and derivation of explicitly testable hypotheses has not yet appeared and is one of the main purposes of this book.

5.3 Comparative Advantage in Aviation

Previous studies have attempted to identify comparative advantage in aviation services. Findlay and Forsyth (1985) applied the comparative cost version while Sapir and Lutz (1981) explicitly drew on the Heckscher-Ohlin theorem. Neither proved terribly persuasive given the present regulatory environment. An interesting point of conflict in these studies is the assumptions made about the capital or labor intensity of producing aviation services. Sapir and Lutz believed that aviation services are physical and human capital-intensive. One can see how this hypothesis is formulated by looking at the large aircraft and highly skilled crew necessary to provide these services. The distinction between comparative advantage and the Heckscher-Ohlin theorem becomes relevant. Many of the inputs used in the production of international aviation services are bought or leased on the international market. They are not restricted by the original factor endowments of the home country. Pilots trained in economically advanced countries fly for airline companies around the world. Generally prices for their services are determined at competitive international rates. Similarly aircraft can be bought or leased at the going global rate. Some variations exist across countries, but differences are small in comparison to the wage differentials for unskilled and semi-skilled labor. To the extent that airlines obtain their inputs on international markets, cost structures across countries would be identical. In this hypothetical situation comparative advantage could only be determined by the cost differences in the production of other products. Exceptions to this indeterminancy could be found in the exploitation of economies of scope due to differing networks or other regulatory distortions causing non-input cost differentials. In short, cost differences of national inputs and differences due to regulation (i.e. unidentical network structures) determine comparative advantage in aviation services. The international mobility of key (particularly capital) inputs makes cursory assumptions about the factor intensity of aviation services subject to question. For these reasons it is quite possible that trade in aviation services may appear to violate the Heckscher-Ohlin theorem, as traditionally formulated. The law of comparative advantage, however, continues to hold, (as does the pattern of trade measured by net factor flows). This is because trade is not based on factor endowment differences but for other reasons, i.e. different abilities to exploit economies of scope.

5.4   Aviation Services and Development

The premise of international civil aviation regulation, the Chicago Convention and the resulting latice of bilateral air service agreements is that traffic generated by a country (like its air space) is soverign property of the state. It is to be shared, traded or monopolized as the soverign nation sees fit. The fallacy of this viewpoint is compounded by its inconsistency with economic efficiency. Passengers travelling by air whose origin, destination or stop-overs causes them to be part of the traffic "generated by a soverign state" may have no other connection with that country. This is increasingly true as traffic and mobility expands on a global scale. Attempts to control or distribute this traffic via air service agreements designating carriers, capacity, fares, or other aspects of service often violates the consumer's soverignty to choose the service which best suits his needs and prevents the airline from providing the best quality service at the lowest cost. An example of the latter is the obstacles air service agreements construct limiting a carrier's ability to create a network of hubs and spokes. This limits the economies of scope available to the carrier, raises its costs and increases the economic cost of providing aviation services to society.

The description of comparative advantage in aviation services combined with the inappropriate argument for allocating passengers as sovereign property leads to interesting thoughts about the role of aviation services in the development process. It is possible, for example that developing countries have a Heckscher-Ohlin style comparative advantage in aviation services if semi-skilled or unskilled labor inputs are the determining factor. Under these circumstances the wage/skill ratio would determine trade in aviation services. This could be true if all other inputs are purchased by airlines at internationally competitive prices. On the other hand, other considerations rather than factor endowments may dominate the determination of comparative advantage for developing countries. Geographical advantages allowing countries to serve as hubs and to take advantage of sixth freedom traffic (e.g. Singapore and Abu Dhabi) may lead to comparative advantage. Regulatory frameworks and resulting networks also contribute to a country's ability to establish successful trade in aviation services. Traffic density access due to location or networking plays an important part in this determination. Other input costs and networking factors limit developing countries' potential comparative advantage in aviation services. Airports and other infrastructural inputs as well as connections via computerized reservation systems (CRSs) with other information networks appear to pose significant obstacles to substantial developing country exports in aviation services. On the whole, Heckscher-Ohlin perspectives of trade in aviation services may lead to the conclusion that (some) developing countries have a comparative advantage relative to labor poor nations. However, factor specificities such as airports, CRSs and low traffic densities may off set these apparent advantages.

The linkages between air transport services and other goods and services, especially when packaged together (e.g. tourism services) adds other considerations. Development issues concerning the provision of adequate air transport infrastructure as an essential component of the development process does not necessarily imply that the services have to be provided by a developing country. Importing these services may be a more rational strategy. Cheaper, more efficient, imported aviation services may promote greater exports of other goods and services. More critical for developing countries is the logical implications of initial levels of low densities. Low densities force airlines serving developing countries to trade flight frequency for efficiency by using smaller, less economical aircraft. Linking larger networks via feeder services may provide the most efficient way to obtain aviation services. Special charter operations offer another alternative for special needs. Charters have worked successfully on the North-South tourist routes in Europe.

On purely economic grounds, developing countries need not subsidize a national airline. Establishing and operating an efficient airline is costly. The basic ingredients include airport infrastructure (runways, terminals, etc.), skilled labor (for management, ticketing, advertising, marketing, ground and air services, etc.), and of course aircraft. Weak demand features often imply expensive operations. Developing countries also face a number of obstacles which exceed these basic cost factors. They are at a disadvantage in negotiating profitable traffic rights in bilateral air service agreements, partially due to weak domestic demand. Thus creation of an effective international network is usually precluded. Limited access to essential computer reservations systems also contributes to more costly operations. The exceptions to these caveats, the rapidly growing countries in Southeast Asia, avoided the pitfalls through clever exploitation of geographical location, skilled labor and, especially in the case of Singapore, a policy open to competition from the outside world. It should be noted that these exceptions are among the cheapest, most efficient producers of aviation services across the globe.

In addition to the fact that setting up a flag carrier may violate the country's comparative advantage, this policy represents a high opportunity cost of the vast resources spent on the airline, related services and infrastructure. Leaders must consider these costs against national security and vital services arguments. Not having a national airline may be an efficient choice and alternative policy actions may exist to accomplich these other policy objectives. The absence of a flag carrier does not imply the absence of aviation services. Importing aviation services would cause a resource reallocation, perhaps into activities which stimulate growth and development.

5.5   Aviation and Some GNS Issues

In the context of the Uruguay Round of Multilateral Trade Negotiations, Group of Negotiations on Services (GNS) questions arise surrounding the application of General Agreement on Tariffs and Trade (GATT) principles to trade in aviation services. At the mid-term review of the Uruguay Round held in Montreal in December 1988 the Ministers (GATT, 1988, p. 40) agreed that

... before the concepts, principles and rules which comprise a multilateral framework for trade in services are finally agreed, these concepts, principles and rules will have to be examined with regard to their applicability and the implications of their application to individual sectors and the types of transactions to be covered by the multilateral framework.

The GNS reviewed aviation with respect to, *inter alia*, the following concepts, principles and rules: transparency, progressive liberalization, national treatment, most-favored-nation/non-discrimination, market access, increasing participation of developing countries, safeguards and exceptions, and the regulatory situation. Although these topics are dealt with in the concluding chapter, here it is important merely to raise the issues. The concluding chapter will elucidate recommendations for policy actions related to these concepts, principles and rules for aviation and especially for the broader category of general trade in services, taking the discussion beyond the Uruguay Round.

Many rules concerning aviation services are transparent. Few hidden barriers to trade exist, except in so far as the rules were designed while ignoring aspects of trade. The challenge comes in assessing the trade impediments represented by rules concerning aviation and related services. Among the barriers would include, but not be limited to, traffic rights; access to airport slots, gates and other ground facilities; discriminatory pricing for fuel or labor; ticketing and CRS practices; rules concerning linkages with tourism related services including restaurants, hotels and car rentals; and any direct or indirect subsidization scheme. Across countries the appropriateness of the rules and barriers will be subject to continuing international discussion.

Progressive liberalization apperars as one of the major objectives of the trade negotitions. Even during the mid-term review, the Ministers foresaw the need for ongoing modalities and procedures which would continue the liberalization process beyond the Uruguay Round. In aviation liberalization implies changes in bilateral air service agreements which adopt measures similar to those in the Bermuda II (i.e. multiple designation, country of origin or double disapproval fares, and break of guage rules). It also means removal of some of the barriers listed in the preceeding paragraph. Progressive liberalization could lead to greater acceptance of fifth and sixth freedom traffic and eventually, perhaps, some cabotage rights. Ideally progressive liberalization would use as its guiding objective a world where aviation services were provided under open skies subject only to health, safety and contestability.

This open skies objective is consistent with national treatment of foreign operators in domestic circumstances. Some problems are presented when domestic carriers are divorced from international operations (as in Australia). If foreign international airlines are treated identically to national airlines, which operate exclusively on international routes and are prevented from operating on the domestic market, then national treatment applies, but an open skies policy does not operate.[6] Similarly an international investor operating a carrier in a foreign country which is limited only to domestic passengers conforms to the same circumstances (i.e. national treatment without open skies).[7] An open skies policy requires the elimination of the distinction between domestic and international carriers. Only then will national treatment truly optimize trade in aviation services.

A most-favored-nation (MFN) or non-discrimination concept as applied to aviation would prevent the creation of aviation services "clubs". In a club only the members could potentially benefit from increased liberalization. As in traditional customs union theory, the creation of a club could be trade creating or distorting depending upon the circumstances of the membership. Club formation is inconsistent with the agreed objectives of the GATT, although in practice MFN principles are frequently violated. The role of networks and economies of scope has implica-

---

[6]Since 1988 QANTAS has been allowed to fly domestic passengers only if they were interlining with an international carrier, (IAC, 1989, p. 112).

[7]This condition will exist in Australia from November 1990, (IAC, 1989, p. 105).

tions for the benefits of MFN as applied to aviation. These implications will be discussed in light of the results in succeeding chapters.

Similar to national treatment, market access crucially affects trade in aviation services. In fact traffic rights and market access are almost synonomous, except when foreign subsidiaries act autonomouosly from the parent company (as in foreign owned domestic carriers). As mentioned above regarding alternative modes of transmission of trade in services, market access via foreign investment can substitute in some ways for enhanced traffic rights.

Previous pages described the role of developing countries in trade in aviation services. One must reiterate that not all developing countries have weak airlines and not all OECD countries have strong ones. As in other service sectors, trade in aviation services is not a North-South issue. However, pursuing comparative advantage will promote a better allocation of resources across all countries. Some countries will be better at producing aviation services, which means cheaper imports of these services for all other nations. This does not conflict with trade practices consistent with promoting growth with equity.

The Ministerial declaration, quoted in part above, mentioned examples of safeguards for balance of payments reasons and exceptions based on security and cultural policy. For aviation services security, ensuring provision of fundamental transportation and prestige obtained via flying the flag on the national carrier consitute the principle exceptions that countries may apply to avoid or delay progressive liberalization. Political considerations may allow these exceptions to weaken any agreement on trade in services. Economists have a responsibility to accept these results but point out the costs and benefits to consumers and producers at national and international levels. The costs of maintaining an inefficient national carrier remain high, as are the costs to the international community of delaying progressive liberalization.

Pervasive regulation in air transportation affects trade in aviation services intentionally and unintentionally. Some moves toward a more deregulated or liberalized regulatory environment have been suggested above. Further comments must draw on the results delineated in the next two chapters. Therefore regulatory issues are broached again in more detail in the concluding chapter.

Chapter 6

Modeling Aviation Services Trade

There are a number of essential economic factors desirable in a trade model of international aviation services. First, the general framework should describe behavior of firms as oligopolistic. Other options such as perfect competition and perfect contestability have been shown to miss essential behavioral and institutional features. Oligopoly will permit the explicit analysis of a small number of actual competitors on any particular route. Second, all of these approaches allow for firms to behave as profit maximizers, a rational economic characterization of airlines. This should not prevent the analysis from considering the effects of subsidization and other support for the national airline.[1] A third important goal for modeling trade in international aviation services is that the model should capture the output effects of economies of scope available from hubbing-and-spoking. Fourth, the model should explicitly derive testable predictions concerning the pattern of trade from these market shares. Fifth, the model needs to show the

---

[1] In correspondence with the author, Mr. T. F. Davies suggests that "Airlines are not solely profit maximizers and that even privately owned airlines consider growth as an important short term consideration — no doubt because it should result in long term profit maximization." This points to a carrier's ability to maintain and expand its output levels over time.

effects of subsidization and other support for the national airline on the trade predictions. Furthermore, it should provide the rationale for eventual consolidation of firms in the sector. Finally, the model should incorporate the influence of deregulation on these predictions. It should be consistent with the observed facts that the initial phase of deregulation causes increased entry, price decreases and output increases. In this chapter a simple model will be developed which more closely reflects the market structure and the key characteristics associated with international scheduled aviation services described above.

6.1   Determining output

The model developed in the following pages follows the style of Brander (1981), Brander and Krugman (1983), and Kierzkowski (1986, 1987b). For simplification and analytical tractability the model is restricted initially to a two airline world, the national flag carriers A and B. Airlines A and B are residents in countries A and B, respectively. However, there are three countries A, B, and C; country C does not have an airline in the initial case. Thus the capital letters A, B, and C refer simultaneously to countries and airlines. Again, the model considers only international services rendered by these airlines on the two markets (between A and B, and between A and C). To avoid the so called integer problem, output is measured in easily divisible revenue passengers actually carried. The difference between the capacity decision of the aviation firm established within the limits of the bilateral agreement and the actual number of revenue passengers carried usually varies widely. Observed load factors of 60-70% warn against the implicit assumption of 100% load factors. The qualitative and intuitive instruction offered by the model concerning the relevance of scope economies for international trade is not affected significantly by such complications, since the output concept used is limited to actual revenue passengers carried by airlines. Defining output in this way also allows its use as a strategic variable. Although capacity controls exist, as described previously, the number of people that an airline carries is more flexible. Strategic decisions can influence output in this sense.

Furthermore, it is assumed that all airlines have access to the same technologies. The total cost functions take the forms consistent with equations which distinguished scale from scope:

$$TC(Z) = c\sum_i X_{Zi} - \sum_j p_{Zj} \times X_{Zj} \qquad (6.1)$$

In other words the total costs of firm Z are a function of the variable costs, c, associated with output of the firm, Z, on each market, i, minus the cost savings due to economies of scope associated with each *pair* of markets, p_{Zj}. (Note that (X_{Zj}) represents some function of outputs by firm Z in two distinct i markets; this function is assumed to be multiplicative.) This cost structure has been selected because economies of scale do not appear to be significant in aviation services, whereas scope economies are suspected.[2] The precise functional form ultimately relies on its simplicity.

6.1.1 Case 1

Specifically, case 1 consists of a situation where the national flag carrier from country A serves both market 1, (between A and B) and market 2 (between A and C), while the airline from B only serves market 1.[3] This is illustrated in Figure 6.1.

Under these circumstances, B has no opportunity to exploit economies of scope, since it only produces one product (i.e. it serves only one market). Thus the total

---

[2]Since equations of profit maximization will rely on output decisions across the entire fabric of routes, scale economies can safely be ignored. For an example of scope and scale in a similar framework see Kierzkowski (1987b).

[3]In Chapter 7 these markets are subdivided into one-way markets for empirical reasons. The definition of a market in this chapter simplifies the description of the model without altering resulting testable hypotheses.

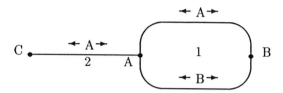

Figure 6.1: **Case 1 Market Structure**

cost functions in this situation take the form:

$$TC(A) = c \times (X_{A,1} + X_{A,2}) - p \times X_{A,1} \times X_{A,2} \qquad (6.2)$$

$$TC(B) = c \times (X_{B,1}) \qquad (6.3)$$

where c and p are assumed strictly positive.

Following Kierzkowski (1987b) assume simple inverse demand functions for the airlines of the form: $P = a - b(quantity\ demanded)$. In equilibrium (the quantity demanded equals the quantity supplied) the inverse demand schedules for markets 1 and 2 can be written as:

$$P_1 = a - b(X_{A,1} + X_{B,1}) \qquad (6.4)$$

$$P_2 = a - b(X_{A,2}) \qquad (6.5)$$

where P_1 and P_2 represent the uniform prices within markets 1 and 2.

Assume that airlines behave as Cournot duopolists. That is, the service output decisions by an airline are based on the assumption that its competitor will keep the level of output chosen in the previous period. In Friedman's (1977, p. 72) words: "the ith firm assumes that all other firms choose in period t the same output which they chose in period $t - 1$."

The three main criticisms of the Cournot style behavioral assumption are well known. Again, as Friedman (1983, p. 42) put it:

First, it is economically unreasonable that the firms would be in a
dynamic environment and not care about future profits. Second, it
is unacceptable to assert that a firm would expect its rival to repeat
today its action of yesterday when, time after time, the other firm had
systematically failed to do so.

The third criticism, of course, is Bertrand's famous complaint that this behavioral
assumption uses quantities rather than prices as the firms' strategic variable.

In response to these criticisms one must note that given non-cooperative behavior, (which airlines usually exude regarding the actual number of passengers
served), the Cournot equilibrium is the maximum level of profit attainable. Second, although learning is expressly prohibited by the model, anticipation of the
other firm's actions would lead to the Cournot solution inevitably and quickly.
Third, choosing quantities rather than prices as the strategic variable is consistent with a recent and careful study by Brander and Zhang (1989). When testing for Cournot, Bertrand or cartel behavior with airline duopoly data from the
United States, they conclude that the Cournot model seems much more consistent with the data. Other studies may chose alternative strategies, however, data
requirements for models using prices as the strategic variable will increase the
difficulty of testing resulting hypotheses empirically. Although other strategies of
Stackleberg-style or of alternative conjectural variations varieties could be used,
the Cournot strategy is simple and is commonly accepted in the field of industrial
organization (and increasingly in international economics).

With this information it is possible to find out which output and price solutions
will equilibrate the system. To accomplish this, note that total profits of A and
B, respectively, are:

$$\pi_A = P_1(X_{A,1}) + P_2(X_{A,2}) - TC(X_A) \tag{6.6}$$

$$\pi_B = P_1(X_{B,1}) - TC(X_B) \tag{6.7}$$

Substituting for P_1 and P_2 from equations 6.4 and 6.5, respectively and for functions $TC(A)$ and $TC(B)$ from equations 6.2 and 6.3, respectively, yields:

$$\pi_A = [a - b(X_{A,1} + X_{B,1})](X_{A,1})$$
$$+[a - b(X_{A,2})](X_{A,2})$$
$$-[c(X_{A,1} + X_{A,2}) - p(X_{A,1})(X_{A,2})] \tag{6.8}$$

$$\pi_B = [a - b(X_{A,1} + X_{B,1})](X_{B,1}) - [c(X_{B,1})] \tag{6.9}$$

Assume that airline companies maximize profit by selecting output levels in each separate market. The first-order conditions are then:

$$\frac{\partial \pi_A}{\partial X_{A,1}} = a - 2b(X_{A,1}) - b(X_{B,1}) - c + p(X_{A,2}) = 0 \tag{6.10}$$

$$\frac{\partial \pi_A}{\partial X_{A,2}} = a - 2b(X_{A,2}) - c + p(X_{A,1}) = 0 \tag{6.11}$$

$$\frac{\partial \pi_B}{\partial X_{B,1}} = a - 2b(X_{B,1}) - b(X_{A,1}) - c = 0 \tag{6.12}$$

Obviously if $b > 0$ then $-2b < 0$. This satisfies the second-order conditions and verifies the existence of a Cournot equilibrium. Linearity and the assumption of strictly positive output values ensure uniqueness of this equilibrium in the positive quadrant. Rewriting gives:

$$- 2b(X_{A,1}) + p(X_{A,2}) - b(X_{B,1}) = c - a \tag{6.13}$$

$$p(X_{A,1}) - 2b(X_{A,2}) = c - a \tag{6.14}$$

$$- b(X_{A,1}) - 2b(X_{B,1}) = c - a \tag{6.15}$$

or in matrix form:

$$\begin{bmatrix} -2b & p & -b \\ p & -2b & 0 \\ -b & 0 & -2b \end{bmatrix} \begin{bmatrix} X_{A,1} \\ X_{A,2} \\ X_{B,1} \end{bmatrix} = \begin{bmatrix} c - a \\ c - a \\ c - a \end{bmatrix}$$

Assume all the parameters are positive, $a > c$ and $b > p$.[4] This ensures that $3b^2 > p^2$. Solving with Cramer's rule one obtains:

$$X_{A,1} = \frac{(a-c)(b+p)}{(3b^2 - p^2)} \qquad (6.16)$$

$$X_{A,2} = \frac{(a-c)(3b+p)}{2(3b^2 - p^2)} \qquad (6.17)$$

$$X_{B,1} = \frac{(a-c)(2b+p)(b-p)}{2b(3b^2 - p^2)} \qquad (6.18)$$

The above assumptions assure economically meaningful results for equations 6.16 through 6.18. Under these assumptions one generally finds that:

$$X_{A,2} > X_{A,1} > X_{B,1} \qquad (6.19)$$

That is, due to the economies of scope, the output decisions of national carrier A in each market in equilibrium are greater than B's output; A serves more than half of market 1. Furthermore, due to the lack of competition, A's output in market 2 is larger than in market 1. Note also that, in the limit, as the economies of scope variable approaches zero the outputs of A and B in market 1 converge, (the result of a simple Cournot duopoly with identical players), while A's output in market 2 remains slightly larger than these outputs.

Although these results may be reinterpreted to fit several kinds of services, they neatly conform to circumstances in international aviation. Market 1 shows third and fourth freedom traffic rights for both airlines. However, A's access to market 2, via similar traffic rights, gives it an edge in market 1. The reasons for this may include the use of the shared inputs located in A to serve both markets and/or the ability to use either route to feed traffic into the connecting routes increasing its load factors (the percentage of seats filled). In other words, the economies of scope obtained by A may derive from any of the shared input

---

[4]These conditions ensure an economically meaningful intersection of supply and demand curves in all markets, even if the supply curve is negatively sloped.

possibilities enumerated previously, and especially from using A as a hub and/or exploiting sixth freedoms of the air.

What happens as the economies of scope parameter shrinks? Although the dynamics of such an adjustment are unspecified, one can compare the resulting equilibria in a comparative static sense. In short, if airlines' abilities to exploit economies of scope diminish, the market structure formalized above yields a more equitable distribution of market 1; A's output diminishes and B's output increases. The results for A's performance in market 2 are ambiguous, as resources are shifted within the company towards the unchallenged market. Of course, inverse results are expected if airlines find ways of exploiting greater scope economies.

Having established the equilibria output solutions, it is now possible to evaluate prices in the various markets. This is easily accomplished by taking the output solutions found in equations 6.16, 6.17 and 6.18 and plugging them into the inverse demand equations 6.4 and 6.5.

$$P_1 = a - \left[\frac{(4b^2 + bp - p^2)(a - c)}{2(3b^2 - p^2)} \right] \qquad (6.20)$$

$$P_2 = a - \left[\frac{(3b^2 + bp)(a - c)}{2(3b^2 - p^2)} \right] \qquad (6.21)$$

Obviously the assumption $b > p$ implies that $P_2 > P_1$. This is consistent with *a priori* expectations since the level of competition in market 1 is higher than in market 2. In contrast with the perfectly contestable markets approach, outlined earlier, using this model shows that the number of firms competing for the market makes a difference.

Calculation of prices allows comparison with average costs to list each firm's mark-up in each market. Define net average revenue (i.e. price minus average costs) as the measure for a firm's mark-up. Applying average incremental costs in cases where a carrier serves more than one market, one obtains the result that relative mark-ups for firms follow output. In other words, larger outputs also imply larger mark-ups. This result holds for all cases explored in the following paragraphs.

6.1.2 Case 2

In the previous case the bilateral service agreement between countries A and C was used only by the A carrier. In the next case consider the start up of a new international airline, the flag carrier from C. The market structure will look like Figure 6.2. What will happen when C serves market 2?[5] This will alter the inverse

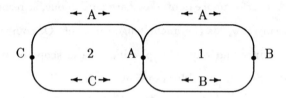

Figure 6.2: **Case 2 Market Structure**

demand equation 6.5 to:

$$P_2 = a - b(X_{A,2} + X_{C,2}) \tag{6.22}$$

It also adds C's new total profit function, which incorporates another total cost function lacking economies of scope.

$$\pi_C = P_2(X_{C,2}) - TC(X_{C,2}) \tag{6.23}$$

As a result, a new set of zero profit conditions can be derived.

$$\frac{\partial \pi_A}{\partial X_{A,1}} = -2b(X_{A,1}) + p(X_{A,2}) - b(X_{B,1}) = c - a \tag{6.24}$$

$$\frac{\partial \pi_A}{\partial X_{A,2}} = p(X_{A,1}) - 2b(X_{A,2}) - b(X_{C,2}) = c - a \tag{6.25}$$

$$\frac{\partial \pi_B}{\partial X_{B,1}} = -b(X_{A,1}) - 2b(X_{B,1}) = c - a \tag{6.26}$$

---

[5]This is equivalent to the situation outlined in Kierzkowski (1987b).

$$\frac{\partial \pi_C}{\partial X_{C,2}} = -b(X_{A,2}) - 2b(X_{C,2}) = c - a \tag{6.27}$$

The results of Cournot behavior are not surprising; the equilibria outputs are somewhat symmetrical:

$$X_{A,1} = X_{A,2} = \frac{a - c}{3b - 2p} \tag{6.28}$$

$$X_{B,1} = X_{C,2} = \frac{(a - c)(b - p)}{b(3b - 2p)} \tag{6.29}$$

Remembering that $b > p$, the right-hand side of equation 6.28 is greater than the right-hand side of 6.29. Economies of scope enjoyed by airline A allow it to fly more passengers than its competitor in each market. Note however that the level of output of A in each market has diminished, (compare equation 6.28 with equations 6.16 and 6.17); concomitantly $X_{B,1}$ has increased (compare 6.29 with 6.18). The reasoning is simple. Entry by airline C reduces A's ability to exploit economies of scope. The ability of C to take away some of the market formerly served by A, forces A's costs up and thereby reduces A's output in both markets.

The symmetry of the output equilibria equalizes prices across markets:

$$P_C = a - \left[\frac{(a - c)(2b - p)}{(3b - 2p)} \right] \tag{6.30}$$

Prices have fallen relative to values P_1 and P_2, (the term in the brackets has increased).

6.1.3 Case 3

These results would be even more symmetrical if B was allowed to compete in market 2 *instead of C*. In this third case, if international aviation was liberalized to allow B this fifth freedom traffic right, the model would become perfectly symmetrical as *both* airlines exploit economies of scope. The market structure will conform to Figure 6.3. The new reaction functions describe a system where output per airline in each market becomes identical in equilibrium,

$$X = \frac{a - c}{3b - p} \tag{6.31}$$

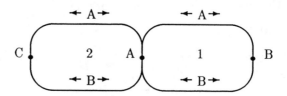

Figure 6.3: **Case 3 Market Structure**

and markets are split evenly. Moreover, prices equalize again:

$$P = a - \left[\frac{2b(a - c)}{3b - p} \right] \tag{6.32}$$

6.1.4 Summary

In summary, output for airline A in market 1 declines as C enters competition with it in market 2 and even more drastically as B enters that second market. When airline B uses economies of scope it is a stronger competitor. Concomitantly, prices decline steadily as one moves from the first situation towards the third example. The important point to emphasize is that *the effects of economies of scope influence an airline's ability to increase output,* $(X_{B,1})_{case1} < (X_{B,1})_{case3}$. In addition, the model shows that *the number of competitors also affects output,* $(X_{A,1})_{case1} > (X_{A,1})_{case2}$. Despite the fact that neither airline B or C exploited economies of scope, the additional competitive pressure from C diminished A's ability to do so and consequently diminished A's output. These two results generalize as new routes are added.

The results lead to several empirical questions. First, does a carrier's output (revenue passengers carried) depend positively on its economies of scope and negatively on the number of competitors in the market? Second, does empirical evidence justify the use of the economies of scope parameter across an airline's entire network or does the evidence suggest that disjoint routes add little (or no) economies of scope to a carrier's ability to capture market share? In other words, should economies of scope be measured across a carrier's network or on a route by route basis? These questions are addressed in detail in the next chapter.

In addition these results may explain the motivation behind the mergers observed in recent years. Expanding an airline's network via mergers increases economies of scope (it may also reduce the number of competitors) and thereby increases output for the acquiring carrier.

6.2 Trade in aviation services

Up to this point the model has not explicitly taken account of international trade in aviation services. Taking the definition of international trade of aviation services, the model's results can be combined with some restrictive assumptions to shed light on trade in these services.

6.2.1 The direction of trade

Look at the trade between countries A and B in case 1. Assume that the countries are identical in every way except for their national flag carriers services. Without differences in relative factor endowments or economies of scale, these assumptions alone would prohibit trade under the Heckscher-Ohlin or contestable markets approaches. However, with economies of scope built into the model, trade still occurs.

To demonstrate this note that the inverse demand function for market 1, (equation 6.4) has remained unaltered throughout the exposition. In other words, prices are uniform in this market. Note that, the assumption made about countries A and B in the previous paragraph implies identical preferences and thus an identical number of residents from A and B will want to fly between the countries. Further these passengers will be perfectly indifferent whether they fly on carrier A or B. Under these circumstances the number of passengers carried by each of the carriers will determine the plausible level of net exports. The net exports of country A on market 1 can be expressed mathematically as follows:

$$netE_{A,1} = \frac{1}{2}(X_{A,1} - X_{B,1}) \times P_1 \qquad (6.33)$$

Half the flying population are B residents and less than half the number of passengers on market 1 can be served by carrier B. Therefore, A must export, on net, some air transport services to B on this market (i.e. A must fly more B residents than B flies A residents). Unfortunately, the extreme nature of these assumptions and the difficulties of disaggregating scarce data (e.g. unavailable observations of net exports per route) prevent direct empirical investigation of this hypothesis.

6.2.2   The extent of exports

Data problems force economists to satisfy themselves with more meager objectives. What level of exports will a particular country experience given the market structure outlined in the model above? Assuming a constant level of imports for simplicity, the answer to the quantity of exports question reduces to a simplified analysis of the pattern of trade.

Equation 6.34 expresses the extent of exports formally:

$$E_{A,1} = \alpha_1 \times X_{A,1} \times P_1 \qquad (6.34)$$

This equation states that the value of country A's exports on market 1, $(E_{A,1})$, equal some constant proportion, (α_1), of the number of passengers carried by A on market 1, $(X_{A,1})$, times the price charged per passenger, (P_1). The constant term represents the proportion of non-A residents flown by carrier A. If, for example, the residency distribution was identical for all airlines flying in a market, then in the example given above, $\alpha_1 = \frac{1}{2}$. It is easy to see that under this assumption, equation 6.34 relates directly to equation 6.33, (i.e. the differece between A's and B's exports).[6]

---

[6]This assumption was not necessary to derive net exports. Take the case where residents

When aggregated equation 6.34 yields:

$$E_A = \sum_i \alpha_i \times (X_{A,i} \times P_i) \qquad (6.35)$$

A's exports of aviation services equals the sum across markets of the weighted products of its output (revenue passengers carried) with the price charged per passenger. The weighting denotes the propensity for non-A residents to fly on the A carrier.

The following chapter develops an empirical test of this relationship. Exports alledgedly correlate positively with the number of revenue passengers carried by an airline across its entire network. In addition to the empirical caveats described in the next chapter, two theoretical points are worth mentioning. First, the value of the α_i's may be determined by preferences, advertising and similar demand factors, as well as the influences of the regulatory environment. One of the criticisms mounted by analysts who have read preliminary versions of these chapters is that the theoretical results may be sensitive to alternative formulations of the demand function. Remembering that for simplicity a simple inverse demand function was specified, alternatives might include Cobb-Douglas or more general Constant-Elasticity-of-Substitution (CES) functions and/or a Lancasterian (1980) demand function which accounts for the various characteristics desired by consumers of aviation services. Other studies of demand for aviation services include variables for income, air fares, flight frequency, delay times, total travel time, airplane transfers, and airline safety, reputation and promotion, (for example see Morrison and Winston, 1989).

The model presented above abstracts from these complex additions, noting that data by international city-pairs for these demand characteristics are unavailable or difficult to find at best. Undoubtedly there exists some sensitivity of the

---

prefer to fly their "home" carrier. Although carrier B, in the limit, will not obtain any exports for country B, A will still export on net according to equation 6.33. Those B residents unable to get tickets on the B airline will have to fly with carrier A.

theoretical results to the vagaries of specific demand features. However, these features may not be uniform across countries and certainly the inverse relationship between demand and air fares (prices) must dominate the list. Future work will determine the degree to which the model formulation above misses these details.

As a second theoretical point, anyone who has flown with a scheduled carrier knows that the assumption of uniform pricing within markets is false. However accurate data on pricing either within or across a carrier's markets presents an intransigent problem. Assuming that airlines merely charge a positive fare, (i.e. they do not pay people to fly), equation 6.35 yields a testable hypothesis. These points should be kept in mind when assessing the empirical findings.

6.2.3 Trade implications of protectionism

As noted in previous chapters, a measure of protection frequently called upon by nations desiring to protect air transport services is the use of subsidization. This method may occur directly or indirectly. Direct payments to the national flag carrier overtly identified as a subsidy does not appear frequently in data reported to ICAO (for example see ICAO, 1986a, 1986b). However, the range of devices effectively subsidizing the national airline grows as one considers the issue. Subsidization for the purposes of this analysis refers to a broad range of protective interventions which prevail in international aviation. Some examples of protectionist practices which fall under this category of subsidization include: discriminatory user charges; favorable government finance; illegitimate discounts, overrides, and rebates; discriminatory taxes; not to mention economic relief associated in some way with government ownership or control.

Subsidization rather than capacity controls are considered for two reasons. First, the non-cooperative output decisions implicitly work within these capacity constraints, which have become less restrictive over time. Second, the hidden nature of subsidization makes an interesting use of the model presented above.

Powerful and pervasive, subsidization is likely to continue especially in a liberalized regulatory environment. The concluding chapter discusses the policy relevance of these points.

The effects of subsidization in the framework delineated above has relevance for determination of outputs and, therefore, international trade. For example, take case 1 where A competes in both markets and B operates solely in market 1. The government in B, realizing that there is no real difference between the airlines and yet observing carrier B's relatively poor performance in market 1, may decide to take matters into its own hands. The pretext may be to support an "infant industry" airline, to protect national esteem, to counter "unfair" competition from A, or any of a number of other reasons. Whatever the rationalization, suppose the B government provides a subsidy to carrier B. Again, for the purposes of the example using the model, the form of subsidization may take any variety. The equivalent of a direct payment may actually occur as a discriminatory landing fees, maintenance servicing, petroleum pricing, or other allocation. What is important is that some branch of the government allows B certain advantages at all levels of output which are prohibited to the other airline.

Formally this may be expressed by subtracting a certain amount per unit output in B's total cost function. Thus combining equation 6.2 with

$$TC(B) = c(X_{B,1}) - s(X_{B,1}) \tag{6.36}$$

and restricting the subsidy, s, to be smaller than c[7], the following output results obtain:

$$X_{A,1} = \left[\frac{(a-c)(b+p) - bs}{(3b^2 - p^2)} \right] \tag{6.37}$$

$$X_{A,2} = \left[\frac{(a-c)(3b+p) - ps}{2(3b^2 - p^2)} \right] \tag{6.38}$$

$$X_{B,1} = \left[\frac{(a-c)(2b+p)(b-p) + s(4b^2 - p^2)}{2b(3b^2 - p^2)} \right] \tag{6.39}$$

---

[7]In fact, it must be assumed that $a - c > s$ for economically meaningful results.

In other words, A's output declines in both markets and B's output increases. Using this equilibrium solution to find the equilibrium price in market 1 gives:

$$P_{1,s} = a - \left[\frac{(a-c)(4b^2 + bp - p^2) + s(2b^2 - p^2)}{2(3b^2 - p^2)}\right] \qquad (6.40)$$

Prices in market 1 have fallen as a result of the subsidy's effect on output in this market. Put another way, B's increased output level more than compensates for A's reduction of output in market 1.

In this specific situation, if the subsidy is adequately large, (such that $2s > a - c$), then B will become a net exporter on market 1. It is possible for B not only to improve its current account position in services against country A but to actually change the sign, i.e. move from a net importer to a net exporter. Regardless of this possibility, it is clear that country B improves its export position against A by using a subsidy.

As Krugman (1984, p. 187) notes for the case of static decreasing costs and complete exclusion of the foreign firm: "Protecting the domestic firm in one market increases domestic sales and lowers foreign sales in all markets." Analogously, the model reaches an identical conclusion in the presence of economies of scope and a domestic subsidy: *import protection is export promotion*. In the model the rise and fall of outputs and prices depend on the price elasticity of demand, the level of the subsidy and economies of scope.

With the subsidy B will gain an additional share of market 1 at A's expense; country B's exports of services improves. This subsidy becomes more interesting if one considers market 2 simultaneously. A's loss in market 1 has a feedback effect on its performance in market 2. B's subsidy, and subsequent achievement of a greater output in market 1, reduces A's ability to exploit economies of scope and thus diminishes the size of market 2.

An odd result develops if one considers case 2, where C participates in market 2. In this case, B's subsidy (through its effects on A's services) improves C's balance of trade in aviation services.

6.2.4   Trade implications of deregulation

The trade implications for deregulation (or the more likely liberalization) of international trade in aviation services follow directly from the model and equation 6.35. Liberalization of international markets, in the first instance, takes place by increased entry. As demonstrated, entry into the market by firms B or C diminish A's output, and thereby, its exports. On the other hand, expansion of A's network into new markets will cause A's exports to increase. Opening markets to increased competition will provide opportunity (and risk) for airlines to expand (or maintain) their output and this will have corresponding effects on the trade of international aviation services. The exact results will depend on the market structures and values of the parameters outlined in the model, including the magnitudes of economies of scope. These issues will be discussed at length in the policy chapter.

6.3   Summary

Some brief remarks are appropriate before moving to Chapter 7, which will empirically test the hypotheses concerning exports and for economies of scope in international scheduled aviation services. Previous attempts at modeling these services have not adequately taken account of market structures or economic characteristics present in this sector. The model described in this chapter attempts to correct for these omissions. In section 6.1 a model of international aviation services using oligopolistic behavior and incorporating economies of scope (without economies of scale) explicitly in firms' cost functions allowed the derivation of market outputs. Three separate cases were analyzed and the results showed that the output of an individual firm depends upon its ability to exploit economies of scope and on the number of competitors in the market. Turning to trade, in contrast with the models of perfect competition or perfect contestability, trade will take place in the model developed in this chapter, even though countries are identical and there are no economies of scale. If the empirical test in Chapter 7 determines that economies of scope, as used in the model, are important in explaining exports of international aviation services, then the implications of the sections concerning subsidization and deregulation given the analysis of the model will serve as a guide to policy making.

Chapter 7

Empirical Research

The purpose of this chapter is to check whether or not the model previously out-lined is consistent with empirical observations. Section 7.1 looks briefly at the correlation between exports of international aviation services and the number of passengers flown by the flag carrier. The subsequent section tests the working hypothesis of the model concerning factors important in explaning the number of revenue passengers carried. The unreliability and scarcity of data on services permeats air transport as well. Perhaps the problems are less profound than in other service sectors, due to the data collection of ICAO and IATA. Nevertheless, the study of trade in international aviation services is not facilitated by readily available and reliable data. The creation of a worthwhile data set has presented innumerable problems. The lack of data tailored to the needs of the following pages requires the use of proxies and necessitated loading of data on a computer by hand. Although much more work on this level inevitably must be done to further the understanding of trade in services, it is hoped that duplication may be avoided. Therefore, within each part of this chapter data sources and cal-culations of each variable are carefully identified and analyzed. As with other areas of trade in services analysis, the data are inexact proxies for the desired variables. This fact will affect the results and implications of the test. The sam-ple includes all countries containing a single flag carrier which reported data for exports and traffic by flight stage in 1985.[1] In all cases ordinary least squares regression techniques were applied using version 4.0 of the Time Series Processor, (TSP) computer package. The regressions illustrate several empirical features of international aviation services. The last section summarizes the results and draws some conclusions.

7.1 Explaining Exports

As outlined in previous chapters, exports of international aviation services measures the value of transporting passengers whose residency differs from the carrying airline. However, the data gathering process prevents precise calculation of these exports. The data used as a proxy for the absolute level of exports of aviation services are taken from the United Nations Conference on Trade and Developement (UNCTAD) database on services "passenger credits" item.[2] The available data list annual figures from 1978 to 1985 for 129 countries in thousands of U.S. dollars. These data follow International Monetary Fund (IMF) balance of payments statistics, where passenger credits are exports of passenger services. This is a subcategory of "other transportation", itself a subcategory of transportation services in the current account. Passenger services record payments of fares, on board expenditures and additional charges for supplementary services (such as excess baggage fees) made to carriers for the transportation of persons. As noted by Sapir and Lutz (1981, p.14), passenger transportation may take place by land, sea, or air; "however, the airline industry dominates the business." To the extent that other modes of transport are used, the data overstate exports of aviation services. Therefore, in general, a passenger credit is awarded to an economy when a foreign resident purchases a travel title (airline coupon) outside

---

[1]The primary data sources are the UNCTAD database of IMF "passenger credits" statistics and the ICAO *Traffic by Flight Stage 1985*, (ICAO, 1986c).

[2]The data, current as of August 3, 1987, were provided by Bruno Lanvin, Office of the Secretary-General, UNCTAD.

the economy's national boundaries. Titles bought by foreign residents within the economy's territory are classified under the "travel" item; thereby excluded from passenger credits. To the extent that foreigners buy their tickets on the domestic carrier while in the domestic market, the passenger credit item will understate exports of airline services. Unfortunately, the noise within this data set is unavoidable, yet to date provides the best information available. Airlines presently do not distinguish between revenues obtained from foreigners and revenues obtained from passengers sharing the carrier's residency. The only way airlines (and thus, governments and the IMF) have to distinguish their revenues is by the location of the purchase. The assumptions maintained by using passenger credits as the dependent variable in the empirical work which follows are that: 1) these credits record airline services only and 2) carriers' foreign sales are to foreigners (i.e. non-residents) exclusively and concomitantly domestic sales are exclusively to residents. Admittedly these are strong assumptions. Nevertheless, given the scarcity of reliable data, they are unavoidable. This is one of the reasons why the results of the emprical work must be considered a first approximation to reality.

To verify the relationship between exports and other measures of airline output, additional data was gathered from *World Air Transport Statistics 1985*, known as WATS, (IATA, 1986a). Of the 22 flag carriers reporting passenger credits and traffic by flight stage statistics (used for subsequent tests), only 17 reported their operations in WATS. The countries which reported include: Australia, Cyprus, Ecuador, Egypt, Finland, Germany, Greece, Indonesia, Kenya, Kuwait, Malta, New Zealand, Pakistan, Philippines, Portugal, South Africa, and Spain. Alternative independent variables of output for each airline included the number of passengers carried (PC), thousands of passenger-kilometers flown (PKF), thousands of tonne-kilometers performed (TKP) and the kilometer length of the scheduled route network (LSRN).

Using passenger credits as the dependent variable, simple linear ordinary least squares regressions were run using only one of the alternative independent vari-

124

Table 7.1: **Export Tests Using WATS Data**

Equation	Constant	PC	PKF	TKP	LSRN	$\overline{R}^2$	No. Obs.
1)	-145793	0.50 **				0.85	17
	(148377)	(0.05)				(451122)**	
2)	-209506		0.16 **			0.70	17
	(229392)		(0.03)			(645221)**	
3)	-190765			1.73 **		0.70	17
	(226343)			(0.28)		(643292)**	
4)	-507095*				9.18 **	0.77	15
	(250165)				(1.31)	(585166)**	
5)	-98275	0.39 **	-0.86	9.32	0.89	0.87	15
	(222707)	(0.13)	(0.51)	(5.43)	(2.93)	(437367)**	

Note: The last column reports the sample size. The regressions containing LSRN as an explanatory variable exclude observations from the Philippines and South Africa, as the data were not reported. The standard errors of the coefficients appear in parentheses below the coefficients and the standard error of the regression appears in parentheses below the adjusted R^2. One and two asterisks by the coefficients show statistical significance (as measured by a standard t-statistic) at the five and one percent level, respectively. Asterisks by the standard error of the regression show similar statistical significance as measured by the F-statistic.

ables at a time. The results in Table 7.1 show that the number of passengers carried performed better than any other explanatory variable. Although all other measures of output correlate with exports positively and significantly at the 99 percent level of confidence, passengers carried (PC) has the most explanatory power. When these independent variables were used in a multivariate regression only PC remained statistically significant. In fact it remained significant at the 99 percent level of confidence. The adjusted R^2 stays approximately the same as in the first equation.

To be consistent with tests conducted later in this chapter a similar test was run using the total number of revenue passengers carried (RPC) as reported in *Traffic by Flight Stage 1985*, (ICAO, 1986c). The difference in independent variables between this test and the first regression equation reported in Table 7.1 relies on the fact that the data are reported and coallated by IATA in the former, while ICAO organizes the information in the latter test. In both instances passengers carried include passengers who pay 25% or more of the normal fare. In principle these data should not differ. However, the IATA figures (PC) were reported in the aggregate whereas the ICAO figures (RPC) were reported by route and aggregated by the author. It is useful to run this sixth test on exports so that the data used subsequently to test outputs remains consistent with the results of this part of the chapter. As noted above, of the 94 countries reporting passenger credits for 1985 only 22 had single flag carriers reporting traffic by flight stage statistics for that year. AVIATECA, the Guatemalan airline, was dropped from the sample since its network caused singularity problems in several subsequent empirical tests described below. The remaining 21 countries/airlines constituting the sample are shown in Table 7.2. The number of revenue passengers carried (RPC) variable was calculated by hand loading on computer the number of revenue passengers carried per route per airline as listed in ICAO (1986c). The data are reported alphabetically for every international station-pair in the world in 1985 and had to be reorganized by airline. The variable RPC simply represents the sum of all the revenue passengers carried by an airline on all of its routes served in 1985. More details concerning this data source will be described below.

The results of this regression closely match the findings of the first equation in Table 7.1, to wit[3]:

6)   Exports=   -259306   +0.47 RPC** $\overline{R}^2 = 0.83$ No. Obs. = 21

                 (146125)   (0.05)   (450225)**

The main distinctions between this equation and the first equation in Table 7.1 include the way in which the data for passengers carried (PC versus RPC) were

---

[3]As in Table 7.1 standard errors appear in parentheses and asterisks connote significance.

Table 7.2: **Countries/Airlines Sample**

Country	Airline Name	Code
Australia	QANTAS	QF
	Qantas Airways Ltd.	
Cyprus	CYPRUS AIRWAYS	CY
	Cyprus Airways Ltd.	
Ecuador	ECUATORIANA	EU
	Compañía Ecuatoriana de Aviación, S.A.	
Egypt, Arab Rep. of	EGYPTAIR	MS
	Egyptian Arab Airways	
Finland	FINNAIR	AY
	Finnair Aero O/Y	
Germany, Fed. Rep. of	LUFTHANSA	LH
	Deutsche Lufthansa AG	
Greece	OLYMPIC	OA
	Olympic Airways S.A.	
Indonesia	GARUDA	GA
	Garuda Indonesian Airways N.V.	
Kenya	KENYA AIRWAYS	KQ
	Kenya Airways	
Korea	KAL (KOREAN AIR)	KE
	Korean Air Lines Inc.	
Kuwait	KUWAIT AIRWAYS	KU
	Kuwait Airways Corporation	
Malaysia	MAS	MH
	Malaysian Airline System Berhad	
Malta	AIR MALTA	KM
	Air Malta Co. Ltd.	
New Zealand	AIR NEW ZEALAND	TE
	Air New Zealand Ltd.	
Pakistan	PIA	PK
	Pakistan International Airlines Corp.	
Philippines	PAL	PR
	Philippine Air Lines Inc.	
Portugal	TAP AIR PORTUGAL	TP
	Transportes Aéreos Portugueses S.A.R.L.	
Singapore	SIA	SQ
	Singapore Airlines Ltd.	
South Africa	SAA	SA
	South African Airways	
Spain	IBERIA	IB
	Líneas Aéreas de España, S.A.	
Sri Lanka	AIR LANKA	UJ
	Air Lanka	

gathered and the sample size. The calculation of RPC may lead to some discrepancies. In general the RPC variable yielded higher figures than PC for the number of passengers carried. Equally important, the sample in the latter equation adds observations for Korea, Malaysia, Singapore and Sri Lanka.

One may interpret the coefficient on revenue passengers carried to mean that an additional passenger carried on average adds approximately \$500 U.S. to exports. At first glance this figure seems reasonable. However, these results must be taken with much caution. One factor potentially mitigating the findings includes the locational definition of exports for recording purposes. As noted above, this may cause the dependent variable to be overstated or understated. Another factor affecting these results comes from the independent variable. As measured, neither the RPC nor the PC variable distinguishes between residents and non-residents, causing overestimation of the number of non-residents. Exports should only include airline ticket sales to non-residents. Put another way, all tickets are assumed to be bought abroad. This biases the coefficient downwards. The proportion of non-residents flown by an airline is unknown and difficult to proxy but probably does not equal 100 percent. (In other words, the α_i term in equation 6.35 probably does not equal one.) The proportion probably varies across countries and across markets. Moreover, under this interpretation of the coefficient, prices in each market are held constant by assumption. Price differences across markets probably influence these results. Expensive long-haul and first class fares are mixed with short haul and economy prices. Additional caveats include the limitation of the data to scheduled international aviation services (which ignores non-scheduled services and alternative modes of transport), and finally but not least, the impact of regulation, pooling arrangements and disguised subsidization. Despite these shortcomings, passenger credits go a long way in describing the variance of passenger service exports.

7.2   Explaining Passengers Carried

The results shown above confirm the intuition of Sapir and Lutz cited earlier. However, the real question remains: how do airlines obtain the number of passengers carried? The following subsection outlines the working hypothesis. Then a subsection discusses why this study does not apply the test for economies of scope found in the work on industrial organization. A subsequent subsection discusses alternative interpretations of the working hypothesis. Description of the data gathering process follows immediately. Finally the section reports and analyzes the results of these tests.

7.2.1   The Working Hypothesis

Having established a relationship between exports of passenger services and the number of revenue passengers carried by an international flag carrier, it remains to develop empirical evidence explaining the number of revenue passengers carried. The model outlined in the previous chapter demonstrated that an airline's output in any given market depends postively on its economies of scope and negatively on the number of airlines serving the market. Moving from a theoretical model to empirical observation, it is necessary to note that the precise number of passengers carried also would depend on the size of the market. Functionally one could describe this as:

$$RPC = F(Scope, NRA, TRPC) \qquad (7.1)$$

In other words, RPC, the number of revenue passengers carried, depends positively on some measure of economies of scope (Scope), negatively on the number of airlines serving the market (NRA) and positively on the total number of revenue passengers carried on the market, i.e. the market size, (TRPC). The model shows the positive scope effects through the assumed form of the cost functions. The negative relationship with the number of airlines on the market results from the market structure of the model. Market size gives the appropriate dimension to this function.

The derivation of this theoretical relationship does not allow explicit specification of the model. Simple linearity is assumed to hold as a good first approximation. Both linear and log-linear equations are run to see which general specification performs better. This point will be expanded when the test results are reported.

7.2.2 Direct Tests for Economies of Scope

Before moving to alternative interpretations of the working hypothesis, exploration of the field of industrial organization which tests directly for economies of scope will cast light on the testing methodology. One way to evaluate the relevance of the model would be to test the airlines' cost functions for economies of scope. As a part of the industrial organization field, investigations of this nature primarily have focused on financial institutions in the United States, (Berger, 1988, Berger, Hanweck and Humphrey, 1987, Kim, 1986, Lawrence, 1989, and Mester, 1987). Kim (1987) performs a similar task for water utilities and Evans and Heckman (1984) use data from the U.S. Bell System. Although this is not the appropriate place to thoroughly review this work,[4] the general thrust and methodology will provide a useful background for the tests outlined below.

Two points are worth highlighting. First, all tests for economies of scope rely on information concerning costs. The estimation of a multiproduct translog cost function, which allows the researcher to determine the existence and magnitude of economies of scope, immediately poses a problem in international aviation services. Cost data are not available for the different routes (products). Obviously the test cannot be conducted without these data.

The second point refers to an advance made in this line of thought by Kim (1986). Kim carefully shows that two different tests for scope economies are appro-

---

[4]Lawrence (1989) outlines some of the methodological developments since the 1960's and emphasizes recent findings.

priate. The first test determines whether the multiproduct cost function exhibits overall economies of scope. This relies on the theory developed in Baumol, Panzar and Willig (1982) showing that cost complementarities between products is a sufficient condition for overall economies of scope. These "cost complementarities imply that the marginal cost of producing any one product decreases with increases in the quantities of all other products", (Kim, 1986, p. 223). For the second test Kim draws on the work of Panzar and Willig (1981) to test for product-specific economies of scope. These economies "... exist when the joint production of an output with the existing combination of other outputs is cheaper than its separate production", (Kim, 1986, p. 223).[5] Inspite of the paucity of cost data, distinguishing overall from product-specific economies of scope has its parallels in the interpretation of the model developed in Chapter 6.

7.2.3   Interpreting the Working Hypothesis

The lesson of the industrial organization work on economies of scope can apply equally well to the working hypothesis described above. The working hypothesis can apply to overall revenue passengers carried across airlines or it can apply to revenue passengers carried on a route by route basis for a particular airline. Stating these propositions another way, an aggregate or overall test for economies of scope in aviation measures the lower costs on any route due to a better overall network structure, while a product-specific test measures the cost effects of inter-linkages with a particular route. This restates for aviation services the dichotomy used by Kim (1986).

---

[5]The interested reader is referred to Kim (1986) who formally distinguishes these economies of scope from overall and product-specific economies of scale. Both kinds of scope economies are consistent with the theoretical discussions in previous chapters.

7.2.4 Data Gathering

The data used to test these various interpretations was derived from the ICAO publication *Traffic by Flight Stage 1985*, (ICAO, 1986c). These statistics break down observations by particular flight sectors and therefore are preferable. Data reporting origin-destination information would disguise the individual sectors and the revenue passengers carried obtained at each stage of the passenger's journey. The data reported by scheduled international operators defines a flight stage as the service of an aircraft between take-off and its next landing. Two cities joined in this way are called a station-pair. Hence, each leg of a voyage is listed separately. The traffic figures list the traffic on-board the aircraft regardless of the passenger's origin or destination. For the purpose of the empirical work, in contrast with the theoretical model already developed, the definition of a market is the one-way trip between two airports. This is redefined because the data are reported in this way and the return voyage (if made) does not necessarily occur under the same circumstances (i.e. with the same number of carriers, market size, etc.).[6]

For each station-pair the following information was extracted and organized by each of the 21 countries/airlines in the sample:

HUB The total number of flights by the airline under consideration into and out of either end point of the station-pair.

NRA The number of reporting airlines is calculated by observing the number of airlines serving one-way on a station-pair and reporting statistics to ICAO.

RPC The number of revenue passengers carried one-way on a station-pair for the airline under consideration. (This variable was aggregated and used in the last export regression equation cited above.)

---

[6]The reader may think of the model as being consistent with this definition of a market by dividing markets as defined in the model into two separate markets as defined in this chapter. This would increase the notation and reduce the simplicity of the model's exposition; however, the results of the model obviously remain unchanged.

TRPC The total number of revenue passengers carried on a station-pair by all reporting airlines.

Due to the lack of appropriate cost data, direct estimates of economies of scope were unobtainable. As a result, one must find a proxy for economies of scope. The variable developed for this could be called "hubness". The number of flights by the same airline which leaves or enters the take-off point and which leaves or enters the landing point for each market was loaded on a computer. Two different "hubness" proxies make sense. Either one accounts for feeder flights into the take-off point plus connecting (onward) flights from the landing station or one takes into account all the routes by the airline in question emminating from and approaching either end of the station-pair. It turns out that the choice between the two does not matter significantly. The reason for this is that, given the general reciprocity and symmetry of bilateral agreements and the need for round trip services, a route into city A from city B is almost always matched by a route in the opposite direction for the same airline. In the limit, when there is perfect symmetry, the first proxy is exactly half as large as the second one. Empirically this would cut the coefficient in half but leave the standard error unaltered. The second alternative was chosen because it accounts for any non-reciprocities. Descriptive statistics for this variable appear in Table 7.3.[7]

The proxy for economies of scope has two advantages. First, it can be used in both the aggregate (overall) and route by route (product-specific) interpretations. Taking the sum of the HUB variable across a carrier's routes yields a reasonable proxy for hubness of the airline. Second, this variable distinguishes, as well as a proxy can, between scope and scale economies. On a route by route basis, the value of HUB is completely independent of the size of the airline or any measure

---

[7]Johnson (1985) also uses this proxy for "networking complementarities" in his test for successful entry into the post deregulation U.S. aviation market. Using a logit model, he finds that "the success of entry on particular routes is dependent upon an airline's previous network structure," (p. 304).

Table 7.3: **HUB Descriptive Statistics**

CODE	MEAN	STD DEV	MINIMUM	MAXIMUM	SUM	VARIANCE
QF	26.74	10.67	6	53	4225	113.79
CY	31.76	13.55	6	45	1620	183.58
EU	15.69	4.37	6	21	565	19.08
MS	53.87	33.96	6	93	6842	1153.36
AY	47.63	33.05	6	86	6716	1092.26
LH	89.12	74.21	6	194	40818	5507.56
OA	41.88	27.48	4	80	6408	755.35
GA	17.66	5.35	5	31	1360	28.67
KQ	22.07	10.57	4	35	1346	111.83
KE	24.34	15.06	6	43	1728	226.94
KU	42.15	28.36	6	79	5522	804.51
MH	18.67	7.49	8	32	1307	56.14
KM	22.79	8.01	6	31	752	64.11
TE	23.25	11.40	6	40	1418	129.89
PK	36.21	20.41	6	77	6336	416.73
PR	23.34	9.71	5	37	1704	94.31
TP	39.52	24.57	7	68	5058	603.59
SQ	38.32	20.67	8	81	7090	427.41
SA	26.06	12.24	6	51	3284	149.87
IB	40.35	25.80	6	92	11057	665.47
UJ	26.89	12.98	6	51	2286	168.60

of its total output. The proxy merely reflects the degree of networking of the station-pair with the rest of the fabric. To the extent that this also reflects the level of joint production, this is a proper proxy.

Representation of the NRA variable also reflects the finding of the model. Monopoly cases are included in this manner so that, as in the model, a monopolist should produce more than a duopolist. The use of RPC and TRPC measure output and market size respectively. RPC is the same variable used in the last export equation. The TRPC variable reflects the reported market size, which is the relevant dimension for the data.

The number of station-pair observations totaled 2674 for all 21 countries in the sample. The number of markets served by any single carrier ranged from 33 (AIR MALTA) to 458 (LUFTHANSA). The data were used as reported despite the fact that airlines occasionally reported statistics which did not conform to the calendar year. Finally it should be pointed out that many of the caveats cited above in the context of the exports equations also apply to estimates concerning revenue passenger carried, especially those problems associated with bilateral regulation, pooling arrangements and subsidization.

7.2.5   Testing the Working Hypothesis

The following paragraphs report the results of regressions based on the alternative interpretations described above. Two different specifications were run:

$$RPC = Constant + \beta_1 HUB + \beta_2 NRA + \beta_3 TRPC \qquad (7.2)$$

$$log RPC = Constant + \beta_4 log HUB + \beta_5 log NRA + \beta_6 log TRPC \qquad (7.3)$$

Theory suggests that the anticipated signs of β_2 and β_5 are negative and the rest are positive. Both specifications were attempted for the overall test and for each of the 21 route by route tests. This subsection is divided into two parts. The first part describes the overall test and the second part outlines the tests run for each airline. Each part analyses the results of the tests. This analysis pays particular attention to the sign and significance of the coefficients, noting whether or not the equations yield results consistent with the main hypothesis derived from the model. It also compares the goodness of fit between the alternative specifications.

The Overall Tests

The two regressions run for the overall test used aggregated data for each of the 21 countries/airlines in the cross-section. The dependent variable, RPC, sums the number of revenue passengers carried by an airline across its entire network in 1985. The proxy for economies of scope also sums the calculation of HUB on each market across an airline's network.[8] The data for HUB appear in the sum column in Table 7.3. Due to the calculation of HUB for a single route, a large measure of HUB on any route, when aggregated, would tend to expand the aggregated figure disproportionately. Think of a city that contains three one-way connecting routes (A, B, and C in Figure 7.1). This implies a value of HUB for the airline equal to twelve — three station-pairs times the routes flown on each pair which are the hub plus its three connecting routes, $(3 \times (1 + 3) = 12)$ — assuming no other city has any other connections. Each of the three markets adds four to the aggregated HUB value. If one more route is added which connects with the hub city (D in Figure 7.1), the value of HUB rises to twenty, $(4 \times (1 + 4) = 20)$. This characteristic combined with the variable's measure of networking distinguishes the overall HUB proxy from a proxy of economies of scale. Connecting a hub with an existing network enormously increases the value of the hub variable. (Imagine the impact on HUB if D itself served as a hub.)

---

[8]An alternative proxy for scope also was attempted. Defined as the number of routes divided by the number of stations served, this proxy did not perform well in either specification. This proxy does not distinguish economies of scale and scope as well as the HUB variable. In addition, the proxy cannot be applied to the route by route tests reported below, since it relies upon aggregated variables. These disadvantages, mixing scope and scale and poorly representing microeconomic phenomena may explain why the proxy performs poorly.

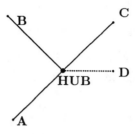

Figure 7.1: **Non-Linear Expansion of "Hubness"**

The NRA variable averages the number of carriers, (the sum of the number of carriers on each market across markets flown by an airline divided by the number of markets served). Using the average number of carriers faced by an airline allows the coefficient on this variable to be more easily interpreted. The coefficient signals the relationship between the number of passengers flown and the degree of competition faced by an airline on average. The total number of carriers on the routes flown by an airline does not contain much information about the level of competition encountered by the airline on its network. It might even reflect a proxy for economies of scale and not the level of competition. The market size variable, TRPC, sums the number of passengers flown by any carrier on the network of the airline in question. As noted above, this adds dimension to the results of the theoretical model.

The results of these regressions are displayed in Table 7.4. In both linear and log-linear cases the sign on TRPC is positive and significant at the one percent level, as predicted. In addition, the coefficient on NRA is negative and significant at the five percent level. These findings are consistent with the *a priori* expectations of the model. The overall economies of scope proxy less clearly indicates evidence consistent with the model. The linear regression strongly suggests that overall economies of scope are present across the sample. However the log-linear specification does not show that the effects of overall economies of scope are significantly different from zero. The fact that the linear regression yields a larger

Table 7.4: Overall Tests

$$\text{RPC} = \begin{array}{cccccc} 1682267 & +75.92 \text{ HUB}^{**} & -609671 \text{ NRA}^{*} & +0.24 \text{ TRPC}^{**} & \overline{R}^2 = 0.84 & \text{SE} = 862037^{**} & \text{No. Obs.} = 21 \\ (928218) & (39.45) & (309895) & (0.06) & & & \end{array}$$

$$\log \text{RPC} = \begin{array}{cccccc} -0.45 & +0.10 \log \text{HUB} & -1.25 \log \text{NRA}^{*} & +0.98 \log \text{TRPC}^{**} & \overline{R}^2 = 0.79 & \text{SE} = 0.39^{**} & \text{No. Obs.} = 21 \\ (2.15) & (0.16) & (0.56) & (0.22) & & & \end{array}$$

Note: See notes for Table 7.1.

adjusted R-squared allows the tentative conclusion that the linear specification is slightly more accurate and therefore, supports the suspicions of the model. However, it is recognized that this is a weak argument to support one regression over another.

The linear regression is interpreted as follows. An airlines's revenue passengers carried increases by approximately 76 for each unit increase of the HUB proxy. As explained above it increases by some multiple of this as the degree of "hubness" increases. On the other hand, an increase in the average level of competition faced by an airline will diminish the total number of revenue passengers carried. An increase of the level of competition by one on average would cause an airline to reduce its RPC by over six hundred thousand passengers. Finally, increasing the total market size of the network by one million passengers would allow a carrier to fly 240,000 more people.

The second regression tells a similar story in terms of rates of change. A one percent increase in the average number of carriers on the airline's network decreases RPC by 1.25 percent. The same percentage increase in the network market size increases RPC by 0.98 percent.

In short, the overall tests find some evidence supporting the hypotheses of positive output effects for overall economies of scope and negative output impacts for increased competition. However, it must be said that the proof of the existence of overall economies of scope is not completely robust.

The Route by Route Tests

Using the data in its disaggregated form allows one to test for product-specific economies of scope and provides an opportunity to see which airlines behaved according to the model. The tests were run country by country, (airline by airline).[9] Each observation for the dependent and independent variables refers to a particu-

---

[9] Attempts to use the entire combined sample failed due to the limitations of the available comupter facilities

lar station-pair. Again, linear and log-linear specifications were estimated. Tables 7.5 and 7.6 display the results from these regressions.

Both specifications were corrected for heteroscedasticity when necessary. A Park-Glejser test for heteroscedasticity was applied by regressing TRPC on the logarithm of the squared error and using the result to make the transformation, (see Pindyck and Rubinfeld, 1981, pp. 150-152).

In general these equations indicate that empirical oberservation is consistent with the model.[10] In the linear case 19 coefficients for the HUB variable were positive and significant at the one percent level and a twentieth coefficient held at the five percent level. The NRA variable had the correct sign in nine cases which were significant at the five percent level or better. Two-thirds of the regressions show TRPC as positive and significant at the one percent level and a fifteenth case held at the five percent level.

In these linear regressions the estimated coefficient for HUB only takes a negative sign in the case of Kenya and does not differ in a statistically significant way from zero. NRA estimates have the "wrong" sign for Ecuador, Egypt, Kenya, Kuwait, New Zealand, Pakistan and the Philippines, although these are never significantly different from zero. Only the Kenyan case yields a negative sign for TRPC and does not differ significantly from zero. Therefore, the signs in these cases are irrelevant.

When significant, the order of magnitude of the HUB coefficient ranges from approximately 10 to 10^3 while NRA ranges around -10^3 and TRPC ranges from 10^{-1} to 10^{-2}. One may interpret each equation as follows. Each connecting route added in either direction to either end of a station-pair adds a number of revenue passengers carried equal to the HUB coefficient to the amount of passengers that airline carries on that international sector. This is typically around 1000 passengers, depending upon the airline. Similarly, an additional competitor on the

---

[10]Alternative specifications, such as semi-log and exponential forms, yield general results similar to those reported.

Table 7.5: **Linear Route by Route Tests**

Country (sample size)	Estimated Coefficients				Statistics	
	Constant	HUB	NRA	TRPC	$\overline{R}^2$	SE
Australia	4257	646 **	-5435 **	0.23 **	0.25	26087 **
(158)	(6418)	(201)	(1515)	(0.04)		
Cyprus	3594	345 **	-4683 **	0.34 **	0.59	17287 **
(51)	(4980)	(119)	(973)	(0.04)		
Ecuador	-15287	1164 **	698	0.05 *	0.22	6546 **
(36)	(7151)	(352)	(499)	(0.02)		
Egypt	-10680 *	302 **	1.83	0.16 **	0.33	18392 **
(127)	(4508)	(50)	(1181)	(0.04)		
Finland[a]	2114	55.85 **	-2207 *	0.18 **	0.04	2110 *
(141)	(1942)	(21.69)	(1107)	(0.03)		
Germany[a]	784	33.37 **	-426	0.26 **	0.18	1176 **
(458)	(967)	(6.29)	(477)	(0.02)		
Greece[a]	456	96.95 **	-1731 **	0.32 **	0.30	977 **
(153)	(1924)	(26.59)	(733)	(0.03)		
Indonesia	-27987 *	2615 **	-2235 *	0.09 **	0.34	25579 **
(77)	(17367)	(565)	(1746)	(0.02)		
Kenya	13064 *	-200	173	-0.00	0.03	15047
(61)	(5435)	(190)	(832)	(0.01)		
Korea	-5062	1402 **	-3857	0.20 **	0.42	36914 **
(71)	(10996)	(306)	(2329)	(0.04)		
Kuwait[a]	-2280	201 **	188	0.04	-0.02	1836
(131)	(2224)	(45.57)	(1112)	(0.02)		
Malaysia	13446	2359 **	-3663	0.13 **	0.24	42422 **
(70)	(16082)	(701)	(2582)	(0.04)		
Malta	-6424	855 *	-1895	0.06	0.14	15183
(33)	(13723)	(460)	(1839)	(0.03)		
New Zealand	-12080 *	780 **	112	0.25 **	0.74	12526 **
(61)	(4900)	(143)	(2250)	(0.04)		
Pakistan	-760	269 **	263	0.01	0.11	16812 **
(175)	(3009)	(63.44)	(651)	(0.01)		
Philippines	-24248	1709 **	1185	0.01	0.17	31306 **
(73)	(13100)	(413)	(1480)	(0.03)		
Portugal[a]	2440	74.62 **	-2287 **	0.28 **	0.22	1388 **
(128)	(1328)	(21.85)	(868)	(0.04)		
Singapore[a]	5154	216 **	-7027 **	0.42 **	0.50	631 **
(185)	(3004)	(66.53)	(966)	(0.03)		
South Africa	349	406 **	-1893 **	0.06 **	0.23	11607 **
(126)	(2970)	(88.73)	(655)	(0.02)		
Spain[a]	5813	108 **	-5361 **	0.49 **	0.60	860 **
(274)	(956)	(19.61)	(454)	(0.02)		
Sri Lanka	6488	227 **	-714	0.01	0.11	9520 **
(85)	(3782)	(93.04)	(496)	(0.01)		

Note: The sample size appears in parentheses below the country's name. The standard errors appears in parentheses below their respective independent variable coefficient. Statistical significance for the constant was based on a two-tailed t-test, since its sign is unknown, a priori. Other significance tests were based on one-tailed t-tests. Two asterisks beside an estimated coefficient denote one percent significance as determined by the t-statistic, while one asterisk denotes five percent significance. Asterisks next to the standard error statistic denote statistical significance determined by the F-statistic. Numbers under 100 were rounded to the nearest second decimal place, while those greater than 100 were rounded to the nearest digit. A value of 0.00 or -0.00 shows a positive figure of less than 0.005 or more than -0.005, respectively.

[a] Denotes equations corrected for heteroscedasticity.

Table 7.6: **Log-Linear Route by Route Tests**

Country	Estimated Coefficients				Statistics	
(sample size)	Constant	log HUB	log NRA	log TRPC	$\bar{R}^2$	SE
Australia[a]	-0.15	0.03	-1.56 **	1.02 **	0.98	0.00 **
(158)	(0.23)	(0.06)	(0.15)	(0.02)		
Cyprus	0.99	0.37	-0.99 **	0.76 **	0.41	1.03 **
(51)	(1.34)	(0.23)	(0.30)	(0.13)		
Ecuador[a]	-2.40	1.14 *	-0.80 **	0.88 **	0.73	0.83 **
(36)	(1.60)	(0.48)	(0.30)	(0.10)		
Egypt	1.54	0.66 **	-0.95 **	0.86 **	0.44	1.34 **
(127)	(1.00)	(0.12)	(0.24)	(0.10)		
Finland[a]	-0.47	0.14 *	-2.18 **	1.00 **	0.82	0.05 **
(141)	(0.25)	(0.06)	(0.18)	(0.03)		
Germany[a]	-1.09 **	0.29 **	-1.14 **	0.98 **	0.34	0.20 **
(458)	(0.24)	(0.05)	(0.10)	(0.03)		
Greece[a]	-1.60 **	0.64 **	-1.65 **	0.92 **	0.49	0.11 **
(153)	(0.52)	(0.14)	(0.24)	(0.06)		
Indonesia[a]	-0.50	0.14	-1.45 **	1.02 **	0.97	0.00 **
(77)	(0.49)	(0.14)	(0.16)	(0.04)		
Kenya	5.20 **	0.02	-0.55 **	0.39 **	0.18	0.73 **
(61)	(0.94)	(0.17)	(0.22)	(0.11)		
Korea	-2.10 **	0.57 **	-1.14 **	1.05 **	0.80	0.66 **
(71)	(0.71)	(0.11)	(0.17)	(0.07)		
Kuwait[a]	-1.10 **	0.52 **	-1.75 **	0.93 **	0.85	0.03 **
(131)	(0.34)	(0.11)	(0.20)	(0.04)		
Malaysia	0.40	0.46 **	-0.88 **	0.84 **	0.71	0.56 **
(70)	(0.84)	(0.17)	(0.11)	(0.07)		
Malta	5.82 **	3.12 **	-1.05 **	0.53 **	0.75	0.97 **
(33)	(2.04)	(0.45)	(0.41)	(0.17)		
New Zealand	-1.63	0.59 **	-0.96 **	0.97 **	0.62	0.76 **
(61)	(1.39)	(0.17)	(0.37)	(0.14)		
Pakistan[a]	0.06	-0.02	-1.52 **	0.99 **	1.00[b]	0.00 **
(175)	(0.26)	(0.08)	(0.11)	(0.01)		
Philippines	-5.98 **	1.70 **	-1.13 **	1.02 **	0.42	1.58 **
(73)	(2.02)	(0.41)	(0.44)	(0.21)		
Portugal[a]	-0.67 *	0.19 *	-1.79 **	1.02 **	0.56	0.07 **
(128)	(0.31)	(0.09)	(0.21)	(0.04)		
Singapore[c]	-2.96 **	0.71 **	-1.52 **	1.04 **	0.49	1.31 **
(185)	(0.95)	(0.18)	(0.20)	(0.09)		
South Africa[a]	-0.03	0.01	-2.41 **	1.00 **	1.00[b]	0.00 **
(126)	(0.12)	(0.04)	(0.12)	(0.01)		
Spain[a]	0.02	-0.14	-1.46 **	1.06 **	0.97	0.00 **
(274)	(0.19)	(0.05)	(0.09)	(0.02)		
Sri Lanka	2.49	0.40	-1.06 **	0.57 **	0.15	1.30 **
(85)	(1.91)	(0.31)	(0.33)	(0.16)		

Note: See notes for Table 7.5.

[b] The adjusted R-squared value exceeds 0.995.

[c] One of the markets was dropped since SIA flew zero revenue passengers on that route.

market will diminish the carrier's RPC on the sector by an amount equal to the NRA coefficient, (also typically in the thousands). An increase in the market size by 1000 passengers typically will only allow the airline to increase its output on that market by some ten to a few hundred passengers.

The log-linear specifications similarly support the model. Almost two-thirds of the coefficients estimated for HUB have correct and significant signs (thirteen, of which three held at the five percent level). In all cases the NRA variable was negative and significant at the 99 percent level of confidence. Similarly, the market size variable displays positive and significant signs at the same level of confidence in all cases.

For the log-linear regressions the "wrong" sign on the HUB coefficient appears only for Pakistan and Spain. These coefficients are not significantly different from zero and therefore their signs are irrelevant. Neither NRA nor TRPC have estimated coefficients with unexpected signs. The orders of magnitude for these coefficients usually range between zero and two in absolute terms for all the parameters. Exceptions to this include Malta's HUB coefficient and NRA coefficients for Finland and South Africa. Frequently the estimated HUB coefficient approximates half the size of the absolute value of the NRA and TRPC coefficients. One exception is the Philippines, where percentage changes in HUB have more impact than equivalent percentage changes in either NRA or TRPC.

To the extent that these coefficients equal one, a one percent change in the parameter for a route causes a one percent change in the airline's revenue passengers carried on that sector. Thus equal changes in the parameters when the values are small (i.e. low hubness, little competition, and /or small markets) cause larger percentage changes in output than when these values are already large.

For the route by route estimates, the log-linear specifications seem to improve the goodness of fit. The adjusted R-squared statistic for the linear regressions ranges from -0.02 for Kuwait to 0.74 for New Zealand, whereas the statistic for the log-linear regressions ranges between 0.15 for Sri Lanka to almost one for

Pakistan and South Africa. The average adjusted R-squared is 0.62 for the log-linear regressions compared with 0.25 for the linear specifications. On a country by country basis, the use of the log-linear specification improves the fit of the regression, (the only exceptions are Cyprus, New Zealand and Singapore). In many instances the fit improves remarkably, especially for Finland, Kuwait and Malta. In the cases of Kenya and Sri Lanka neither specification provides a powerful explanation of variance in the dependent variable. Restrictive bilaterals, pooling, and other market distorting regulations and obstructive conditions could lie behind this phenomenon.

These equations are analytically attractive. Besides the improvement in fit, measuring in percentage terms places the various important factors influencing a carrier's revenue passengers carried in perspective. The percentage increase in product-specific economies of scope generally has less than half the impact of an identical percentage change in market size. Changing the number of carriers per route has more impact as one approaches a lower level of competition, since the percentage changes increase. In other words, as one moves generally from a monopolistic market to a duopolistic market the negative impact strongly affects output compared with change from 33 to 34 carriers in the market.

The route by route test also provide evidence consistent with the model. The log-linear regressions show product-specific economies of scope to have a positive effect on output at the route level in fewer cases than the linear regressions. Nevertheless, under both specifications these product-specific economies of scope clearly influenced a majority of those airlines tested in 1985. The empirical observations for the effects of the level of competition also support the model outlined in Chapter 6. Even though the linear tests show this less often, the log-linear tests imply that the impact of an oligopolistic market structure is stronger when the number of competitors on a market is small (since the percentage changes are large). This fits a priori expectations concerning the degree of competition.

7.3   Summary and Conclusions

The chapter analyzes some empirical findings to determine whether observations consistently coincide with the model described in Chapter 6. Section 7.1 found that the number of passengers carried by a flag carrier correlates positively and significantly with the passenger credit exports of its home country. Intuition and evidence leads to this conclusion. To export more passenger services a carrier needs to serve more people. In the next section both overall and product-specific economies of scope were evidenced. However, these economies do not appear to be universal, as the results in the last subsection point out. Similarly the level of competition on any given sector influences the performance of airlines in that market. Although the absolute number of carriers on a route sometimes impacts a carriers revenue passengers carried, the percentage change of competition universally affects output for the sample under study. The route-by-route log-linear regressions suggest that the true functional relationship is a constant-elasticity of substitution function in the variables described above. However, as noted, data limitations prevent the use of cost data and the estimation of a multiproduct translog cost function. In any case, the results presented above are consistent with the suspicion of the importance of economies of scope.

the choice of empirical specifications remains arbitrary. Due consideration was given to testing alternative functional forms, (see footnote 10). The debate among econometricians concerning the usefulness of Box-Cox transformations and the intricacies of nested reset testing among alternative specifications leads the analysis unnecessarily down the path of interesting but technical econometric controversy. Regardless of the fact that there may exist a better functional form for estimation, which these econometric test might yield, teh results illustrate the essential points. Revenue passengers carried are statistically significantly correlated negatively with increases in competition and positively with available market size and economies of scope. In future work econometricians can determine the extent to which precise estimates of these influences differ from the results reported above. Nevertheless, the policy implications outlined in the next chapter will remain unaltered by econometric improvements omitted here.

The evidence suggests that the hypotheses based on the model be maintained. The degree to which these factors affect any individual airline depends on circumstances. Some airlines, (such as OLYMPIC, TAP AIR PORTUGAL and SIA) conform more closely to the expectations based on the model than others (i.e. KENYA AIRWAYS and AIR LANKA). Despite the prevalence of regulation and other market distortions, the model leads to reasonable conclusions about international aviation services.

These points are even more important in light of the analysis accomplished in the first part of this chapter. The nexus between a country's exports of passenger services and the number of revenue passengers carried by the national airline clearly holds. The empirical work showing the functional relationship between these RPC, on the one hand, and the HUB, NRA and TRPC on the other lead to some trade implications. The indirect link between these latter variables and exports needs little explanation. When a direct empirical linkage was attempted using export figures for all 21 country/airlines from the first part of this chapter and the overall data from the second part, the following results obtained[11]:

7) Exports= 946744 + 75.95 HUB ** - 333623 NRA * + 0.06 TRPC *
            (546153)   (23.21)   (182339)   (0.03)

$\overline{R}^2 = 0.78$ SE = 507213 ** No. Obs. = 21

Given the assumptions listed within this chapter, increasing the degree of hubness or the market size and reducing the level of competition on the routes

---

[11]Asterisks represent statistical significance as noted in previous tables, (see the note to Table 7.1.)

flown by the national carrier will tend to increase the nation's exports of aviation services. The next chapter analyzes the trade policy implications suggested by this conclusion.

Chapter 8

Policy Conclusions

Previous chapters outlined facts, developed a model and tested the resulting working hypotheses. The present chapter draws policy relevant conclusions from this work. The number of subjects approached increases the difficulty of the task. For this reason the chapter is separated into two divisions: aviation policies and trade policies. The first section analyzes the results of preceding chapters for the aviation sector. Different perceptions could cause airlines policy-makers, national governments and regional governors to draw dissimilar conclusions. These may be contrasted with a global welfare maximizer's ideal. The relevant lessons for deregulation and subsidization occupy the major part of this discussion. Reflecting earlier results, important points concerning mergers, computerized reservations systems, airport congestion and safety are discussed. These topics also relate to the theme of reregulation, which is addressed in this context. The policy implications for trade in aviation services begins the next section on trade policies. Again the themes of deregulation and subsidization assume important roles. In addition, the trade policies of developing countries and the impacts of progressive liberalization on these countries receives special attention. Discussion of the Uruguay Round of Multilateral Trade Negotiations Group of Negotiations on Services outlines the principles, rules and concepts relevant to trade in services in the light of the theoretical and empirical results appearing in earlier chapters. Subsequently the section explores the significance of the results for the global trading system beyond the Uruguay Round. It also alludes to the implications for other service sectors such as telecommunications and finance.

8.1 Aviation Policy

Several studies have analyzed the U.S. experience with aviation deregulation and concluded that positive economic welfare effects result, (McGowan and Trengrove, 1986, Morrison and Winston, 1986 and 1989, OECD, 1988, Pryke, 1987, and Sawers, 1987). When these studies considered the possibility of expanding deregulation to the interntional scene, they support the idea, projecting similar welfare benefits internationally. Although the better studies concomitantly identify the practical impossibility of complete international deregulation, all studies wholeheartedly support steps towards more liberal bilateral air service agreements. In this light the following paragraphs outline the kinds of instruction preceding chapters provide concerning greater international liberalization of the airways.

8.1.1 Limits to Scope

A hasty conclusion that could be drawn from the evidence shown above is that airlines should maximize their economies of scope by blindly building multiple hubs and by reducing every possibility of competition. This may be a successful strategy for some airlines, however, there are at least four kinds of limits to economies of scope.

The interesting constraints to economies of scope fall on the supply side. First, not every point on the aviation map can become a hub. Reversion to direct flights between every point to create an infinite number of hubs inefficiently allocates resources, which explains the development of the hub-and-spoke system.[1]

---

[1] An anonymous referee correctly describes this inefficient network as displaying "diseconomies of scope".

Second, bilateral air service agreements most severely limit the potential to exploit scope economies. In addition to specifying points, the bilaterals also determine traffic rights available to a carrier, (including fifth and implicit sixth freedoms). Thus, an effective hub-and-spoke network in the international context relies almost exclusively on the bilaterals obtained.

A government attempting to maximize the economies of scope exploited by its flag carrier may consider excluding competitors from any international traffic on routes emanating to or from its territory. Under the present bilateral latticework of air service agreements, domestic traffic rights (cabotage) are often reserved for the flag carrier. In other cases domestic traffic cannot be flown by any international carrier, unless interlining with a connecting international flight. In situations where domestic traffic is reserved for the flag carrier, economies of scope derived from domestic the traffic enhance the flag carrier's competitive position. Taking advantage of this strategic linkage between domestic and international aviation services relates to the extraction of monopoly rents by the flag carrier. Bilaterals negotiated and approved by governments pursuing this strategy ignore the costs of these actions. Protection of the flag carrier in this manner lowers competition and could raise the costs of the service to consumers (even if the cost savings due to economies of scope were passed on to the consumer). This is because the policy inhibits more efficient airlines from providing these services more cheaply to domestic customers and costs the consumers of other countries to suffer higher prices elsewhere, due to restrictions on the other airline's opportunities to expand their economies of scope and to reduced competition. From this perspective the strategic linkage between domestic and international markets means that a country supporting its flag carrier as a monopoly will increase the costs to travelers across the world and reduce global welfare.

The effects are worse than these phrases indicate, because general equilibrium effects have thus far been overlooked. When one accounts for the general economic impacts by considering aviation services as an input into the production of a number of other goods and services in the economy, higher prices for aviation services has negative effects that filter throughout the economy. The adverse pressures on the various sectors of the economy demonstrate the non-optimal shift of resources towards the protected aviation sector. Moreover, a rent extraction policy by one country reinforces these harmful economic consequences to the extent that other countries pursue a similar strategy in retaliation for its protectionist stance.

Returning to the discussion of limits to scope, the preliminary evidence described in Chapter 7 illustrates the third point that the choice of connecting flights matters in the development of economies of scope. Developing independent spokes will not increase overall economies of scope as much as further linkages among of a key number of hub stations. The fabric of the network must interlink at crucial points for these economies to effect a carrier's output optimally.

An additional series of supply side constraints to economies of scope result from the limitations of international airports. A hub airport easily looses flexibility. Landing and take-off slots and gates become scarce, particularly around popular hubbing-and-spoking hours (i.e. early mornings and late afternoons for business traffic). As traffic becomes heavy air traffic controlers and other general airport facilities rapidly get overloaded. In short, hub airports have to deal with congestion problems. Moreover, the number of airports cannot expand quickly. It takes 10-15 years to plan an international airport and not many are in the pipeline. It is generally accepted that airport congestion will remain an increasingly irritating problem in the future.

Parenthetical to the limits of economies of scope, the role of computer reservations systems (CRSs) cannot be forgotten. The information provided by a CRS is not limited to prices and flight schedules but encompasses information on the entire package of services sold by a travel agent (including tickets, accomodation, ground transportation, etc.). Only a few CRSs exist to effectively serve travel agents due to the high costs of CRS development and the expense travel agents must incur to learn to use a system or to change from one system to another. Major CRSs include: AMERICAN AIRLINES' SABRE; UNITED AIR-LINES' APOLLO; GALILEO being developed jointly by BRITISH AIRWAYS, KLM, SABENA, ALITALIA and others; AMADEUS being developed by AIR FRANCE, LUFTHANSA, SAS and others; and ABACUS being developed by SIA, PAL, MAS, CATHAY PACIFIC, CHINA AIRWAYS and ROYAL BRUNEI. At present some carriers also maintain their own CRS, (e.g. FANTASIA for QANTAS and KRISCOM for SIA). UNITED AIRLINES' cooperation with the GALILEO endeavour strengthens its potential market power. Other possible linkages are in the foreseeable future.

Bias in a CRS creates market power beyond the mere concentration of systems available in the market. Although attempts have been made in the United States at first by the CAB and later by the Department of Justice to ensure that these biases have been eliminated, the issue is not yet resolved. The information yielded by a CRS is critical to an operator's effective yield management (shuffling points of sale and seat availabilities by fare category). Equitable access to a CRS by airlines other than the CRS developer is another issue which may become pertinent for antitrust watchdogs. CRSs can limit or tremendously expand an airline's ability to exploit scope economies. Perhaps the best way to state this point is to note that in the future, hubbing-and-spoking alone will not permit effective exploitation of economies of scope unless linked with an appropriate CRS.

8.1.2 Deregulation

Deregulation experience in the United States led, in the first phase, to rapid market entry by old and new carriers, along with concomitant air fare reductions, increased variety of services and pressure for airlines to become more efficient. The model in Chapter 6 consistently describes this phenomenon. Entry by airline B, (an old airline), or C, (a new airline), results in similar effects. Perhaps the most important consequence of deregulation in the U.S. and the main event unforeseen by those favoring and critiquing regulation alike, was the development of hub-and-spoke networking. Partially caused by the necessity for efficiency and partially caused by firms' desire to expand output for short- and long-run profitability, this new emphasis on the development of the hub-and-spoke network irreversibly changed the airline business. Again the model captures the rationale for hubbing-and-spoking by linking this networking with economies of scope. As described in the model and evidenced in the empirical section, increased economies of scope leads to greater output of revenue passengers carried. The second phase of the deregulation experience finds support from these facts. Possibly as a consequence of hubbing-and-spoking, as well as other economies of scope resulting from the freedom of airlines to act in a deregulated environment, observers of recent events in the U.S. aviation service sector find consolidation of airlines through mergers and take-overs. This has led to increased price discrimination and decreased service quality as carriers abuse their increased market power. These latter events do not lead to an argument for reregulation nor do they suggest that policy-makers should regret deregulation. As Alfred Kahn (1988) evaluated the situation, the gains outweigh the losses inspite of the negative surprises during this second phase of deregulation. However, these events do call for an appropriate form of regulation described below.

On the other side of the Atlantic the trends towards liberalization gathers steam. What do the results outlined in previous chapters recommend for European aviation? The situation in the U.S. differs from the European arena. Immediately the question of liberalization of European aviation takes on international dimensions. Differences in location, and geographical and market size sharply differentiate the two regions. In the U.S., American carriers almost exclusively feed huge domestic traffic into international routes. In Europe domestic monopolies control this behind gateway feed to international services. These domestic monopolies restrict competition and lower the potential economies of scope for the region. This lowers the efficiency of aviation services.

The most efficient way to organize European aviation is to liberalize the market structure as much as possible. The experience in the U.S. underlines this implication. Liberalization is not an easy process. As the 1992 goal of one internal market puts pressure on the aviation sector, the significance of this policy change will need clarification. The analysis in previous chapters shows that liberal policies, if effective, would cause turbulence in the provision of these services. Increased entry and exit would result and the network structure of airlines would adjust to exploit more economies of scope especially via hubbing-and-spoking. The pressures on European aviation could come from several different sources. Charters allowed to compete for business traffic, as well as long-haul, low cost Asian carriers, and strong North American airlines with large domestic feeds and significant economies of scope all could make important incursions into the European scheduled markets.

Europe possesses an advantage over the United States. Calls for reregulation founded on fears raised by mergers and acquisitions or a highly publicized aviation accident can be met early. The second phase of consolidation and monopoly abuses can be avoided through anti-trust regulations and enforcement. These appropriate regulations could be designed to build and maintain a market structure more closely resembling competition rather than oligopoly. The use of contestability as a benchmark would not prevent monopoly on certain routes but would counter monopoly power abuses on all routes. The U.S. experience shows that a perfectly contestable market does not result automatically after the removal of regulatory controls. (It certainly does not exist under present regulatory regimes.) Appropriate policies will promote at least a minimum level of entry and only regulations mindful of the necessary conditions to enhance competition.

There is an appropriate role for regulation, but its role is not to stringently control all aspects of aviation services and it certainly is not to control entry, pricing or other commercial operations unless threatened by anticompetitive circumstances. Pro-competitive policies ensure safety standards and consumer protection and do not interfere with route choice, scheduling and other business operations. It is worth remembering that the trend towards greater safety in air transportation was unbroken by the dramatic changes occurring in the wake of deregulation. In fact, given the large increase in traffic and pressures placed on air traffic controlers and other infrastructure, the ever improving safety record can be deemed remarkable. Therefore, reregulation cannot be argued on the grounds that safety has suffered due to deregulation. It does require that safety standards already on the books must be adequately enforced. Funding of the enforcement agencies must not suffer regardless of the presence of absence of other regulatory measures. Equitable access to hub airports at peak hours can be acheived through economic mechanisms of allocation. Due consideration by airport authorities to promote a competitive environment goes hand in hand with assessment of the economic efficiencies (for producers and consumers) associated with improved aviation networks. The balance to be struck is delicate but essential. These policies should result in a net welfare gain for consumers and producers in the region, enabling a more efficient provision of aviation services to spread globally. Judging by recent European Council Regulations (1987c and 1987d) and Directives (1987a and 1987b) the EC has a long way to go before reaching these welfare maximizing objectives.

8.1.3   Subsidization

Noting the historical relationship between airlines and governments and the theoretical results of government control and protectionism under the guise of subsidization in previous chapters, subsidies allow carriers to increase output and can have a ripple effect through strategically linked markets. An optimal policy from the national viewpoint would use subsidies and/or similar protective devices up to the point of equating the gains from increased subsidization with the opportunity costs. The calculation of this level of subsidization is clouded by other considerations such as: 1) the fact that domestic residents fly on both the national carrier and foreign carriers, 2) the amount of rent-seeking resources expended by the aviation sector in competition with other sectors of the economy for these protective benefits, 3) the value, if any, of having a strong flag carrier for purposes of national defense or self-esteem, and 4) the threat of retaliation which could counteract the effects of subsidization.

This policy is solely optimal from the national and not the global point of view. Global wefare maximization probably diminishes as subsidization increases. Simple application of the theory of the second best leads to the conclusion that the only economically proper subsidization compensates for distortions obstructing the efficient exploitation of economies of scope. Other interventions cause supplementary distortions. If a subsidy is called for in the face of regulation it is probably more efficient to dispose of the regulatory distortion.

Unfortunately in a liberalizing environment, governments may rely more heavily on subsidization. As an easily hidden policy and with a multitude of possible specific instruments enacting similar effects, protectionism may increase even in a liberalizing environment. This is primarily due to the non-tariff barrier character of subsidization combined with the lack of a multilateral accord limiting recourse to such actions. This underlines the importance of multilateral initiatives designed to maximize global welfare and counter inefficient but politically appealing national policies. The following section draws conclusions from the present study for trade in aviation and other services, incorporating discussion of multilateral efforts for progressive liberalization in trade in services.

8.2 Trade Policy

The danger of exaggerating the results and overemphasizing the sector under study presents itself in the following analysis. Thus the reader is cautioned in advance that the policy implications outlined below rely on the results obtained in the previous chapters as well as the authors reasoned prognostication of obtainable results for aviation and other service sectors. Only future work will determine whether empirical observation supports the analytical logic described in subsequent paragraphs.

8.2.1 Aviation Trade Policy

The suspicion in Chapter 6 that exports of passenger services rely on the number of people flown found empirical support in Chapter 7. Chapter 7 generally leaned in favor of the supposition that the percentage of passengers flown by a particular airline on any market depends in a statistically positive way on the number of flights by that airline which linked with that city-pair. These tendencies appear inspite of preponderant international and domestic regulation.

The previous section outlined the policy recommendations for aviation based on the findings, however it omitted direct consideration of the implications for trade in aviation services. The nexus between revenue passengers carried and exports implies that the trade policy implications closely follow the preceeding aviation policy recommendations. Protecting the domestic market from foreign penetration prevents other carriers from developing hubs in the domestic market and exploiting economies of scope. As a result foreign carriers will produce lower levels of output than would otherwise occur under a liberal environment. Low output implies, *ceterus paribus*, smaller exports than under a liberal regime. The prevalence of protected markets also suggests that the "domestic" carrier will have equal difficulty developing hubs overseas. In short, trade is restricted.

This results from all types of restrictions on trade in aviation services. For purposes of analysis there are two kinds of restrictions. First, domestically imposed discriminatory measures inhibit the rendering of foreign aviation service. These devices include: 1) discriminatory user charges for airports and airways as well as user charges at international airports to cross-subsidized domestic services; 2) cheap government finance or government guarantees for otherwise more expensive or unobtainable private finance; 3) regulations preventing or only allowing domestic firms to discount, override, or rebate; 4) limited access regarding CRSs (e.g. LUFTHANSA's monopoly on the START CRS); and 5) other discriminatory practices against foreign carriers. These additional domestically imposed costs may offset the savings associated with building an overseas network. This prevents the optimal exploitation of economies of scope and diminishes the level of trade. The second form of restriction falls into the international category. Restrictive bilaterals limiting traffic rights and points of entry and exit prevent trade from reaching optimal levels. Collusion through pooling arrangements also lowers trade in aviation services.

The forceful economic argument for gains from trade apply almost as universally in the new theory of international trade with imperfect competition as in the traditional framework of trade under perfect competition. To obtain these gains when economies of scale or scope are involved it suffices that trade (as opposed to autarky) leads to an increase in production by the firm exploiting these economies. Therefore, policies that eliminate both forms of restrictions ennumerated above promote trade and improve welfare. Liberalization in aviation will not only lead to the benefits of improved efficiency noted in the previous section, but also implies benefits from the gains from trade. In other words, an additional motive behind liberalization of international aviation services comes from the welfare improvements associated with the greater exchange in these services. The same caveats as above concerning safety and anti-trust regulation and enforcement hold. Appropriate regulation based on competition and full exploitation of economies of scope should lead to policies optimizing trade in aviation services.

Unilateral liberalization involves political difficulties. Aviation often plays a role in national prestige, security as well as affording an opportunity to extract monopoly rents for those involved directly in the provision of aviation services. However there is some recent eveidence to suggest that unilateral liberalization does improve national welfare. Norman and Strandenes (1990) show that domestic welfare increases if a domestic[2] route is liberalized, even if the competition comes from a non-domestic entrant.

Of course the ideal objective of an open skies policy probably necessitates international effort. Agreement on a multilateral scale, under such fora as the Uruguay Round, could move towards creating the political climate needed to achieve this objective, shifting the onus away from brave unilateral action. However, it must be remembered that liberal bialterals or multilateral agreements are only as liberal as market actors actions permit. Collusive behavior (in the presence of deregulation and bilaterals allowing competitive conditions) still violates the spirit of these policy initiatives. Therefore policies must also be established to promote efficiency and competition. Liberalization of aviation and other service sectors is discussed below in the context of the Uruguay Round Group of Negotiations on Services, after a brief exploration of the implications relevant to developing countries.

8.2.2   Development Policies

In many cases developing countries with small aviation markets do not have the density on domestic or international linked routes to support even one commercially viable airline, let alone a competitor. The only rational solution, therefore, is to integrate the market more closely through international linkages and allow other international (non-resident) carriers to enter. Developing countries can reap the benefits of competition and entry in this way.[3] For example the northern part of a country may obtain entry from an airline based to the north and the southern portion of the country may get competition in aviaiton services from a southern neighbor. Small niche markets could remain for competing feeder services. Poli-

---

[2]The Norman and Strandenes (1990) study draws on the case of the Oslo-Stockholm route, which may be considered a domestic route given the structure of SAS.

[3]This advice applies to all small countries, not just developing countries.

cies designed to gain from trade in aviation by buying the cheapest, most efficient services available also release scarce resources to allow the country to pursue its comparative advantage. This does not preclude developing countries from pursing comparative advantage via aviation services exports. However, the implication is that not all developing (or other) countries that have a national airline should do so. Removing the protective regulations that support these inefficient airlines is consistent with an economic strategy for development.

As a rationale for trade, economies of scope is a managerial aspect of economic organization with which trade policy makers and negotiators in developing countries should be, concerned. Exploitation of economies of scope may not be limited to service production, even though it seems that many service activities potentially involve the shared input requirement. Therefore trade in services negotiators and other policy-makers should make themselves aware of this potential reason for trade, particularly those nations whose trade pattern based on other rationales has not led to rapid growth. This refers to countries whose trade primarily takes place with nations of similar endowment and without exploiting significant economies of scale. If a nation possesses the potential to exploit, or indeed already exploits, some economies of scope, then its negotiators will be interested in seeking a trading regime in services that is as liberal as possible. This does not mean that other nations should be correspondingly protectionist, although one can envision that kind of unfortunate political reaction. The point to underline is that by adding another reason to trade to the growing list, (i.e. comparative costs and increasing returns to scale[4]) nations have a way of pursuing their international commerce that violates the natural endowment or the technical production methods available. This results because, as shown earlier, comparative advantage holds for trade in services as it does in goods, but the Heckscher-Ohlin framework may not be relevant. In other words, nations can strive towards increasing their

---

[4]It is important to remember in this context that Helpman (1981) has shown that these reasons to trade are not mutually exclusive.

gains from trade and not be restricted by nature's inequitable distribution nor by the uneven development of technological know-how. To accomplish this goal, however, will require that such nations exploit economies of scope by managerial skill that optimizes potential joint production.

Other development implications of economies of scope also should be noted. The concept relates directly to the Hirschman (and Myrdal) concepts of forward and backward linkages (backwash and spread effects). Cheaper joint production due to economies of scope (especially in services) may allow firms linking with one of the inputs, either in a forward or backward direction, to allow these economies to spread to other economic activities. Thus, economies of scope provide another rationale for pursuing a development policy consistent with this development approach (see Weisman, 1983).

8.2.3   The Uruguay Round GNS

The increasing importance of trade in services and the related negotiations finds support in the General Agreement on Tariffs and Trade (GATT, 1989) annual report. This document reiterates the facts described previously. Services comprise up to two-thirds of gross domestic product for all countries, including developing countries. More staggering are the facts that services trade has grown faster than goods trade (by about two and one-half times). Since 1970 services trade growth has been around 15 per cent per annum. In 1987 services trade exceeded the value of trade in textiles and clothing, was almost twice as large as trade in iron and steel, and was equivalent to the value of world trade in food and fuels, or automotive and electronics exports. The GATT report also emphasizes the role services play in the globalization of the world economy and in the efficiencies gained in distribution and production.

Since the announcement of Part II of the Ministerial Declaration of September 1986, the Uruguay Round Group of Negotiations on Services, (GNS), has struggled with numerous issues of conceptualization, data accumulation and rule-making. The mandate outlined in the Declaration (GATT, 1986, p. 5) states :

> Negotiations in this area shall aim to establish a multilateral framework of principles and rules for trade in services, including elaboration of possible disciplines for individual sectors, with a view to expansion of such trade under conditions of transparency and progressive liberalization and as a means of promoting economic growth of all trading partners and the development of developing countries. Such framework shall respect the policy objectives of national laws and regulations applying to services and shall take into account the work of relevant international organizations.

The present analysis of trade in services strikes at the heart of the trade in services negotiations. The discussions of regulation and protective barriers to trade in services found in previous chapters apply to these important issues in the GNS. The implications for the GNS include discussions of transparency, regulation, national treatment, the most-favored-nation principle and subsidization. Before turning to the subject of regulatory regimes, it is important to discuss the nature of barriers to trade in services under the heading of transparency.

Transparency

The Punta del Este Declaration quoted above notes that the GNS should design a multilateral framework promoting services trade expansion under conditions of transparency. Unlike trade in goods, where tariffs principally obstructed trade when negotiations began, obstacles to trade in services often appear as non-tariff barriers, (NTBs). In fact, one of the possible origins of the trade in services debate stems from the increasing use of NTBs as tariffs on goods diminish.

Trade in services underlines the need for trade policy officials to recognize the weakness of the Heckscher-Ohlin model's policy implications. Contrary to

Mundel's (1957) findings for trade in goods, services trade does not perfectly substitute for trade in factors. An optimal allocation of resources with free trade in goods and services occurs only when factors and goods and services are mobile. Otherwise the provision of some services internationally may occur under a sub-optimal (more costly) mode of transmission. The inefficiency must cause a global welfare loss. In other words, the key to a successful Uruguay Round negotiation on trade in services must address the temporary mobility of labor and capital to complete transactions. The issues have been discussed primarily in terms of rights of establishment (principally capital movements), frequently opposed by developing countries. In response developing nations have raised the issue of labor mobility between nations. The temporary relocation of people must allow greater flows of both skilled and unskilled labor across national boundaries. In theory, specifying temporary movement of capital and labor distinguishes these movements from investment and migration. The practical definition of temporary movement, however, may blur this distinction. Despite the political complexities, only complete mobility of labor and capital (even on a temporary basis) ensures the optimal expansion of trade leading to economic growth and development.

In some cases service transactions require the physical proximity of the producer and the recipient. A barrier to trade in such a service merely must prevent those involved in the transaction from meeting. However, a variety of modes of service transmission avail themselves to the two parties. If the service transaction can occur via another mode of transmission, without direct physical contact, then the barrier to trade diminishes in importance. In fact the barrier disappears when the choice among alternative modes of transmission involves no change in the cost of the service to either party. In other cases the barrier may have some influence on trade. It may also be important to determine who must bear the brunt of any cost differences involved in the choice of transmission. Not only will this affect the pattern of trade but it may also affect the total and distributional assessments of welfare.

The pressure by free traders to limit NTBs in goods leads directly to their limitation concerning trade in services. A first step towards NTB reductions has been labeled the inventory approach (see Hindley, 1986, pp.15-16). Under this proposition governments notify GATT, the body of registration, of any measures which obstruct trade. The principle mechanism allows registered NTBs to continue in the first instance, i.e. they are "grandfathered". Unregistered discriminatory measures are subject to challenge and adjudication via dispute settlement procedures. This approach provides for a standstill of NTBs. Gradually, registered measures become subject to challenge and adjudication. This provides for the eventual rollback of protectionism caused by NTBs and an incentive to avoid the creation of new barriers. Although this inventory approach may provide a mechanism for the reduction of protectionism in trade in services, it does not ensure the elimination of discrimination due to regulatory regimes. Problems will also arise when regulations are created or altered for purposes other than for their effects on trade.

Regulation

The subject of regulation and services trade policy divides into two separate topics. Competition among different regulatory regimes constitutes the first topic. The discussion of regulation in aviation services led to the distinction between domestic and international regulation. For services trade policy different kinds of domestic regulation also carries some importance. The second topic addresses the difference between regulation of goods and of services. In particular it discusses the regulation of entry into a service sector. These topics provide a good introduction for the section on subsidization.

Regulatory Competition Different countries often impose different regulatory requirements on the same services. This causes problems for trade in these services. Questions arise as to whether a service firm from country A should be able to sell services to residents in country B when these regulatory regimes differ. If country A's regulations are more stringent than B's, the firms established in A may have a higher quality but also a higher price. Firms in A may be disadvantaged in their exports to B if quality is not a concern or if they must maintain A's standards even if located in B. On the other hand, B firms may encounter difficulty in providing services to quality conscious A residents or if they have to meet A regulatory standards, (Hindley, 1986, pp. 18-19). There is competition between these regulatory regimes to enhance the export position of resident service firms. These issues simultaneously entertain interesting questions concerning the right of establishment.

One of the early motivations for bringing trade in services into multilateral trade negotiations came from the desire by aviation and financial firms to break into new markets, (Feketekuty, 1988, pp. 299-300). Mere market presence by service firms through licensing agreements, franchises, management contracts, subcontracting and representation offices does not compare with the level and quality of market penetration provided by marketing, sales, and distribution offices, as well as the relocation of personnel overseas. Regulation against foreigners includes entry barriers (discussed below), exclusion from the provision of certain services, ownership limitations, local content or value-added requirements, employment restrictions, and profit repatriation impediments. National treatment for all firms would eliminate the discriminatory nature of these regulations within any given country. Placing all firms on equal footing while subjecting them to the regulatory exigencies deemed necessary by national authorities would diminish some of the barriers to services trade. However, even national treatment would not eliminate the problem of competing regulatory environments across countries. Differences among competing regulatory regimes clearly influence decisions concerning establishment.

The discussion of competition between regulatory regimes begs the question of regulatory coordination. Attempts to harmonize regulatory regimes (e.g. within the EC), are notoriously difficult. The motivations for regulation do not stem solely from economic concerns; they often rely on political reasoning and rarely do they consider trade issues. In the area of financial services the EC has made great progress by calling for mutual recognition of regulatory regimes. Clearly this achievement does not resolve the problem of harmonization in all services. For example, this strategy brings little to promote the liberalization of aviation services. To the degree that airlines conform to the rules and standards of ICAO and the countries with which they have contact, mutual recognition is unnecessary. Progress beyond the regulatory restrictions imposed through ICAO and bilateral agreements must come from supranational rule-making.

The question has been posed whether or not multilateral rules in the GNS should supersede or conform with existing international arrangements (Nayyar, 1989). Clearly the expertise amassed by the sectoral organizations (e.g. ICAO, ITU, UNCTAD, WHO, WTO, etc.) must be used in the design and application of the general concepts, principles and rules in the Multilateral Framework Agreement on Services. The Cooke Committee which coordinated prudential standards in a multilateral setting at the Bank for International Settlements provides an example. However, sectoral groups (e.g. IATA) tend to promote self-interest over national and global welfare considerations. As a result, competition and efficiency considerations at a multilateral forum should guide (and at times supersede) agreed international rules. An umbrella of concepts principles and rules (including transparency, national treatment and most-favored-nation status) should consistently guide the sectoral accords leading to concrete progressive liberalization promoting trade and development.

An additional point concerns the role of the international regulatory environment. Noting the dichotomy between domestic and international regulatory regimes, international regulation contributes to the difficulty of regulatory coordination. Not only do different domestic regulatory regimes need harmonization, but these steps must create or conform to harmonious international rules within which domestic regulatory systems can function. The suggestion here is that minimum international standards be set to ensure the smooth functioning of the market. As with aviation services, other services must conform to minimum safety and environmental standards. The international regulatory regime should encourage undistorted market outcomes to the extent possible. Use of the competition or the contestability benchmark, depending on the market structure and specifications of the service sector, can serve as a starting point for international rule-making.

Regulation of Entry Regulation abounds in goods and services trade, yet manifests itself differently. As Hindley (1987, p. 12) succinctly puts it,

> In goods trade ... the object of regulation is very often the product itself, rather than the producer. In service industries, where products are often less standardised, it is producers rather than products that are usually the object of regulation.

The previous analysis underlines the fact that both kinds of regulation are possible for services. Regulation of producers frequently leads to the control of entry into the industry. This can take the form of a ban or limit on the right of establishment,[5] or some other quantitative restriction such as licensing or capacity controls. The results presented earlier imply that these measures prevent the optimal allocation of resources and restrict the optimal level of trade. Both cause welfare losses to the nation and to the world. The losses potentially occuring due to unnecessary limits to the exploitation of economies of scope should be of particular concern to developing countries. These restrictions prevent the creation of comparative advantage described above. Countries having to rely on the creation of comparative advantage via the development of economies should encourage liberal efforts permitting their exploitation. Again, international agreement to

---

[5]Note that the right of establishment used here implies the relocation of either capital or labor.

regulation based on efficient market functioning could remove the losses incurred as a result of present regulations.

Subsidization

Hindley (1987) suggests that the welfare propositions developed for trade in goods applies in general to trade in services. He concludes that subsidization of output is superior to a tariff, which in turn is superior to a quota. The theory of the second best, upon which much of this analysis is based, shows that an optimal intervention directly attacks the distortion to be corrected. The difficulty lies with the political nature of many policies implemented in the realm of services, as well as the diversity of forms that these interventions take.

The model outlined in Chapter 6 shows that subsidization distorts output. This implies a trade distortion. However, analysis of different kinds of subsidization was not undertaken. It may be that these interventions cause fewer distortions than other measures, i.e. regulation preventing entry. In this case the policy suggestions described above take priority over the elimination of subsidization. Careful study of the various welfare and distributional effects of different kind of subsidies should follow once an inventory of these instruments has been made. A standstill on these distortions should not be seen as a longer term goal. In Hindley's (1986, p. 25) words, "To act to avert a threat to freedom of transaction where such freedom already exists, however, while laudable, can hardly be described as liberalization."

8.2.4   Beyond the Uruguay Round

The Uruguay Round will culminate in December 1990 with formal legal agreement. Although the Multilateral Framework Agreement on Services (FAS) must still resolve several serious negotiating points at the time of writing — including mechanisms for exchanging concessions leading to progressive liberalization, and precise definitions delineating sectoral and country coverage (Dunkel, 1990) — hope exists for a positive conclusion to the four year exercise. Regardless of the outcome, the establishment of rules and implementation of procedures will not allow trade in services to fall off the international agenda as a resolved issue. Continuing debate will extend to the degrees and limits of concepts, rules and procedures, especially those relating to progressive liberalization and dispute settlements.

The participation of developing countries may take several forms in these discussions. At one extreme developing countries will act as equal parties to the FAS. On the other extreme special and differential treatment may exclude these nations from the obligations while granting conditional rights. Application of a conditional most-favored-nation principle could act to weaken the agreement. Liberalization of barriers to trade in services will be difficult for many nations, not only for developing countries. Political will to make necessary regulatory adjustments, to coordinate these changes internationally and at the same time to protect their citizens from potentially unsafe, environmentally damaging or other harm while promoting national objectives will continue to occupy even the most effective governments. Special and differential treatment for a select number of countries reduces these pressures. At the same time it allows inefficiencies to develop which inhibit economic growth and development. These inefficiencies become more difficult to eliminate over time. Drawing on the results outlined in earlier chapters, special and differential treatment can reduce the potential for exploiting economies of scope and simultaneously lower the level of competition, making the provision of services more costly to the consumer and producer. In cases where public ownership is involved, these policies could also exacerbate problems concerning the government budget deficit. In this light any application of special and differential treatment must take into account the economic costs of limiting or delaying the progressive liberalization agreed to by other members of the international trading community.

Fear exists that if the FAS (or any other part of the Uruguay Round) fails to keep the global trading system on the path of multilateral agreement then many economically powerful countries will resort to bilateral methods. The United States of America has played with these options concomitant with the Uruguay Round negotiations and some believe that these methods have met with success. Destruction of the multilateral trading system has grave implications. A result may be the establishment of competing trading blocks with the U.S. - Canada Free Trade Agreement constituting the core of the North American block; 1992 Europe, EFTA and the opening of eastern Europe at the center of another block; and Japan leading the Asian newly industrializing economies and perhaps the Tasman Sea countries in the creation of a third block. The triad of trading blocks flys in the face of the benefits derived through a multilateral trading system founded on the most-favored-nation principle. Without the MFN, powerful countries or blocks could extract favorable trade concessions from trading countries, lowering global economic welfare (and perhaps the standard of living of countries poorly supported by a counter-balancing block). To avoid this dismal scenario the Uruguay Round must be seen as a success. In addition it must establish rules and procedures for improving trade conditions, settling disputes and advancing further discussion in trade in services as in other areas of the Round.

On the optimistic side, given a successful Uruguay Round, future work may lead to the creation of a true International Trade Organization similar to the organ envisioned by negotiators near the conclusion of World War II.[6] The Uruguay Round needs to set the way for future trade negotiations. As the most comprehensive trade round since the ITO discussions in the 1940's, the mandate is to broaden the scope of the international trade regime to areas previously exempt from the rules. This task cannot be accomplished in four years. The Uruguay Round contains the foundations for future work, but much remains for "Uruguay

---

[6]The Services World Forum has already co-sponsored the first meeting on the topic of an International Trade Organization in Geneva in May 1990.

II".

8.2.5   Trade in Services

The implications of the analysis of aviation for other service sectors relates directly to both instruction regarding domestic policies and the Uruguay Round. Many services share characteristics common to aviation. The trend from regulation towards deregulation in services has often led to increased copetition, development of improved networks, and consolidation via mergers and acquisitions. Questions of reregulation sometimes arise in response to increased concentration in the service sector. These circumstances apply not only to aviation, but also to finance and insurance, telcommunications, and other transport sectors. With the exception of government and professional services, these three categories cover most fundamental service activities. They are also critical to the prosperity and development of any viable economy.

Note that the establishment of networks and nodal points or hubs are common in finance and telecommunications as well as transport. The concept of economies of scope readily applies. Cost saving through joint production processes implies that deregulation can expand the exploitation of economies of scope. Domestic policies which prevent the full exploitation of these scope economies, through obstacles blocking information or other network fabrics, penalize consumers and raise the costs of service provision. The joint production process is not limited to simple sectoral considerations. Many services, such as tourism or professional services, use transport, telecommunications and/or finance as part of their output package. Economies of scope derived by multiple services bundled as a single product achieves similar results as the networks in individual sectors. Of course this applies equally to bundles which incorporate goods and services together.

Economies of scope also provide a rationale for mergers and acquisitions, since larger more efficient production (service rendering) results from agglomeration. In an oligopolistic market structure the concentration of a market which limits competition can have some detrimental impacts. The benefits of economies of scope must be weighed against the costs of decreased competition. At this juncture it is appropriate to reconsider regulation. Immediately one must realize that the criteria and rationale for regulation does not lead to control of entry, prices or output, but attacks the potential limit to competition created by concentration. Mere concentration does not pose a welfare problem in a perfectly contestable market structure. The contestability benchmark provides an appropriate first check to see if policies are needed. If the conditions for perfect contestability are met then no interference becomes necessary. Otherwise steps to create perfect contestability are in order. On the other hand, if the conditions of perfect contestability cannot be met, (as in the case of aviation services in the short run due to airport and other constraints), then competition policies, which also account for efficiency gains from economies, should be implemented. The important point is that reregulation means the institution of anti-trust policies which apply to all forms of economic activities. Variously described as competition or trade practices laws, pro-competitive action remains the optimal solution for abuses of market power.

The implications of the results described here for trade in aviation services for the provisions to be outlined by the GNS have parallels in other service sectors. Liberalization promotes economies of scope, which make service production more efficient and promotes trade leading to growth and development. Trade in financial and telecommunications services has revolutionized the global economy. Many gains have been made as a result of the competitive push given by deregulation trends. Limits to scope will differ across sectors, however the concerns may appear similar to aviation. In addition, safety, environmental concerns, prudential standards, equal access to networks and other caveats must limit the extent of liberalization and concomitant economies of scope. Appropriate regulation, such as anti-trust measures, must conform to the establishment of incentives consistent with competition. The difficulties of enacting the changes needed to gain greater efficiency and competition are formidable, however the potential improvements to global welfare make the effort worthwhile.

Bibliography

[1] Alistair Tucker Associates. (1981) "Discriminatory and Unfair Practices and Protectionism in Civil Aviation and their Effects upon the Growth of Air Transport in Developing Countries", a study prepared for the United Nations Conference on Trade and Development, (UNCTAD), February.

[2] Andreu, Narciso. (1987) "A European View of the Airline Industry Today", *ICAO Bulletin* 42 pp. 19-23.

[3] Arndt, H. W. (1989) "Trade in Services with Special Reference to ASEAN", *ASEAN Economic Bulletin* 6(1) pp. 1-30.

[4] Ascher, Bernard and David L. Edgell. (1986) "Barriers to International Travel: Removing Restrictions to Trade in Services and Tourism", *Travel & Tourism Analyst* October, pp. 3-13.

[5] Bailey, Elizabeth E. (1986) "Price and Productivity Change Following Deregulation: The U.S. Experience", *Economic Journal* 96 pp. 1-17.

[6] Bailey, Elizabeth E. (1985) "Airline Deregulation in the US: The Benefits Provided and the Lessons Learned", *International Journal of Transport Economics* 12 pp. 119-144.

[7] Bailey, Elizabeth E. and Ann F. Friedlaender. (1982) "Market Structure and Multiproduct Industries", *Journal of Economic Literature* 20 pp. 1024-1048.

[8] Bailey, Elizabeth E. and David R. Graham. (1985) *Deregulating the Airlines* (Boston: MIT Press).

[9] Bailey, Elizabeth E. and John C. Panzar. (1981) "The Contestability of Airline Markets During the Transition to Deregulation", *Law and Contemporary Problems* 44 pp. 125-145.

[10] de Bandt, Jacques. (1989) "Can We Measure Productivity in Service Activities", in Albert Bressand and Kalypso Nicolaïdis (eds.) *Strategic Trends in Services: An Inquiry into the Global Service Economy* (New York: Harper & Row Publishers), pp. 277-96.

[11] Barrett, Sean D. (1987) *Sky High: Airline Prices and European Deregulation* (Aldershot, United Kingdom: Avebury).

[12] Baumol, William J., John C. Panzar and Robert D. Willig. (1982) *Contestable Markets and the Theory of Industry Structure* (New York: Harcourt Brace Jovanovich, Inc.).

[13] Baumol, William J. and Robert D. Willig. (1986) "Contestability: Developments Since the Book", *Oxford Economic Papers* 38 supplement, pp. 9-36.

[14] Beach, Charles and James MacKinnon. (1978) "A Maximum Likelihood Procedure for Regression with Autocorrelated Errors", *Econometrica* 46 pp. 51-58.

[15] Beesley, M. E. (1986) "Commitment, Sunk Costs, and Entry to the Airline Industry: Reflections on Experience", *Journal of Transport Economics and Policy* 20 pp. 173-190.

[16] Berger, Allen N. (1988) "Review of *Bank Costs, Structure, and Performance* by James Kolari and Asghar Zardkoohi", *Journal of Money, Credit and Banking* 20 pp. 283-287.

[17] Berger, Allen N., Gerald A. Hanweck, and David B. Humphrey. (1987) "Competitive Viability in Banking: Scale, Scope, and Product Mix Economies", *Journal of Monetary Economics* 20 pp. 501-520.

[18] Bhagwati, Jagdish N. (1987) "Trade in Services and the Multilateral Trade Negotiations", *World Bank Economic Review* 1 pp. 549-569.

[19] Bhagwati, Jagdish N. (1986) "International Trade in Services and Its Relevance for Economic Development", Xth Annual Lecture of The Geneva Association held at the London School of Economics and the Graduate Institute of International Studies, Geneva. Published by the *Services World Forum*, (Geneva: Pergamon Press).

[20] Bhagwati, Jagdish N. (1984) "Splintering and Disembodiment of Services and Developing Nations", *The World Economy* 7 pp. 133-143.

[21] Bittlingmayer, George. (1985) "The Economics of a Simple Airline Network", Science Center Berlin, International Institute of Management, mimeo.

[22] Borenstein, Severin. (1989) "Hubs and High Fares: Dominance and Market Power in the U.S. Airline Industry", *RAND Journal of Economics* 20(3) pp. 344-65.

[23] Brander, James. (1981) "Intra-Industry Trade in Identical Commodities", *Journal of International Economics* 2 pp. 1-14.

[24] Brander, James and Paul Krugman. (1983) "A Reciprocal-Dumping Model of International Trade", *Journal of International Economics* 15 pp. 313-321.

[25] Brander, James and Barbara J. Spencer. (1985) "Export Subsidies and International Market Share Rivalry", *Journal of International Economics* 18 pp. 83-100.

[26] Brander, James and Anming Zhang (1989) "Market Conduct in the Airline Industry: An Empirical Investigation", unpublished mimeo.

[27] Bressand, Albert and Kalypso Nicolaïdis, (eds.) (1989) *Strategic Trends in Services: An Inquiry into the Global Service Economy* (New York: Harper & Row Publisher).

[28] Brunker, David, Christopher C. Findlay and Peter J. Forsyth. (1989) "Comparative Advantage in Airline Services" unpublished mimeo presented at the Australian National University, Canberra, Australia.

[29] Buchanan, James M., Robert D. Tollison and Gordon Tullock. (1980) *Toward a Theory of the Rent-Seeking Society* (College Station: Texas A & M University Press).

[30] Cairns, Robert D. and Dhanayshar Mahabir (1988) "Contestability: A Revisionist View", *Economica* 55 pp. 269-76.

[31] Carey, Susan and Julie Wolf. (1987) "EC Adopts Modest Steps Toward Airline Deregulation", *The Wall Street Journal* 8 December, p. 5.

[32] Castle, Leslie and Christopher C. Findlay, (eds.) (1988) *Pacific Trade in Services* (Sydney: Allen & Unwin).

[33] Caves, Douglas W., Laurits R. Christensen and Michael W. Tretheway. (1984) "Economies of Density Versus Economies of Scale: Why Trunk and Local Service Airline Costs Differ", *Rand Journal of Economics* 15 pp. 471-489.

[34] Caves, Douglas W., Laurits R. Christensen and Michael W. Tretheway. (1980) "Flexible Cost Functions for Multiproduct Firms", *Review of Economics and Statistics* 62 pp. 477-481.

[35] Caves, Richard. (1962) *Air Transport and Its Regulators: an Industry Study* (Cambridge, MA: Harvard University Press).

[36] Civil Aviation Authority. (1984a) *Airline Competition Policy* CAP 500 (London: CAA).

[37] Civil Aviation Authority. (1984b) *Deregulation of Air Transport: A Perspective on the Experience in the United States* CAA paper 84009 (London: CAA).

[38] Clark, Colin. (1951) *The Conditions of Economic Progress*, second edition, (London: Macmillan).

[39] Council of the European Communities. (1987a) "Council Directive of 14 December 1987 on fares for scheduled air services between Member States (87/601/87)." *Official Journal of the European Communities L 374*, 30, 31 December, pp. 12-18.

[40] Council of the European Communities. (1987b) "Council Directive of 14 December 1987 on the sharing of passenger capacity between air carriers on scheduled air services between Member States adn on access for air carriers to scheduled air-service routes between Member States (87/602/87)." *Official Journal of the European Communities L 374*, 30, 31 December, pp. 19-25.

[41] Council of the European Communities. (1987c) "Council Regulation (EEC) No 3975/87 of 14 December 1987 laying down the procedure for the application of the rules on competition to undertakings in the air transport sector." *Official Journal of the European Communities L 374*, 30, 31 December, pp. 1-8.

[42] Council of the European Communities. (1987d) "Council Regulation (EEC) No 3976/87 of 14 December 1987 on the application of Article 85 (3) of the

Treaty to certain categories of agreements and concerted practices in the air transport sector." *Official Journal of the European Communities L 374*, 30, 31 December, pp. 9-11.

[43] Deardorff, Alan V. (1985) "Comparative Advantage and International Trade and Investment in Services", with a comment by Ronald W. Jones, Discussion paper No. 5, Fishman-Davidson Center for the Study of the Service Sector, the Wharton School, University of Pensylvania. Appearing in edited form in Robert M. Stern (ed.), *trade and Investment in Services: Canada/U.S. Perspectives* (Toronto: Ontario Economic Council), pp. 39-71.

[44] Dick, R. and H. Dicke. (1979) "Patterns of Trade in Knowledge", in Herbert Giersch (ed.), *International Economic Development and resource Transfer* (Tübingen: J. C. B. Mohr), pp. 335-67.

[45] Dixit, Avinash. (1984) "International Trade Policy for Oligopolistic Industries", *Economic Journal Conference Papers* 96 (Supplement) pp. 1-16.

[46] Dixit, Avinash and Victor Norman. (1980) *Theory of International Trade* (Digswell Place, Welwyn: Cambridge University Press).

[47] Dixit, Avinash and J. E. Stiglitz. (1977) "Monopolistic Competition and Optimum Product Diversity", *American Economic Review* 67 pp. 297-308.

[48] Djajić, Slobodan and Henryk Kierzkowski. (1986) "Goods, Services and Trade", The Graduate Institute of International Studies, Geneva, mimeo.

[49] Doganis, Rigas. (1985) *Flying Off Course: The Economics of International Airlines* (London: George Allen & Unwin).

[50] Dunkel, Arthur (1990) Address by Arthur Dunkell, Director-General, General Agreement on Tariffs and Trade, Geneva, Switzerland, to the Sixth

Conference of Coalition of Service Industries, entitled "A Private Sector Forum on Marketing Services in the 1990's", hosted by the Australian Coalition of Service Industries, Sydney, May 3-4.

[51] Eaton, Jonathan and Gene M. Grossman. (1986) "Optimal Trade and Industrial Policy Under Oligopoly", *Quarterly Journal of Economics* 101 pp. 383-406.

[52] *The Economist.* (1987) "The Beginning of the End for Europe's Airline Duopolies", 21 March, pp.71-72.

[53] Ehlers, P. Nikolai. (1988) *Computerized Reservations Systems (CRSs): How to Optimize the Passenger Benefits* (Deventer, Netherlands: Kluwer Law and Taxation Publishers).

[54] Evans, David S. and James J. Heckman. (1984) "A Test for Subadditivity of the Cost Function with an Application to the Bell System" *American Economic Review* 74 pp. 615-623.

[55] Feketekuty, Geza. (1988) *International Trade in Services: An Overview and Blueprint for Negotiations* (Cambridge, Massachusetts: Ballinger Publishing Company).

[56] Fellner, W. J. (1949) *Competition Among the Few: Oligopoly and Similar Market Structures* (New York: Alfred A. Knopf).

[57] Findlay, Christopher C. (1988) "The Aviation and Tourism Sectors: Recent Developments and Prospects for Regulatory Reform", presented to the Conference on "Australian and New Zealand Perspectives on Japan's Role in the Pacific", Australia-Japan Research Centre, Australian National Unversity, Canberra, Australia, December 9.

[58] Findlay, Christopher C. (1985a) "Effects of Australian International Air Transport Regulation", *Journal of Industrial Economics* 34 pp. 199-210.

[59] Findlay, Christopher C. (1985b) *The Flying Kangaroo, An Endangered Species?* (Sydney: Allen and Unwin).

[60] Findlay, Christopher C. (1985c) "A Framework for Services Trade Policy Questions" Australia-Japan Research Centre research paper No. 126.

[61] Findlay, Christopher C. (1985c) "The Persistence and Pervasiveness of the Regulation of International Trade in Civil Aviation Services", *Singapore Economic Review* 30 pp. 77-89.

[62] Findlay, Christopher C. and Peter J. Forsyth. (1985) "International Trade in Airline Services" Australia-Japan Research Centre research paper No. 123.

[63] Findlay, Christopher C. and Peter J. Forsyth. (1984) "Competitiveness in Internationally Traded Services: The Case of Air Transport" ASEAN-Australia Working Papers No. 10. ASEAN-Australia Joint Research Project, Kuala Lumpur and Canberra.

[64] Fisher, Allan G. B. (1939) "Primary, Secondary and Tertiary Production", *Economic Record* 15 pp. 24-38.

[65] Friedman, James W. (1983) *Oligopoly Theory* (Cambridge, MA: Cambridge Press).

[66] Friedman, James W. (1977) *Oligopoly and The Theory of Games* (Amsterdam: North-Holland Publishing Company).

[67] Galibert, Alain and Jean Pisani-Ferry. (1985) "La théorie des échanges de services", *Economie Prospective Internationale* 22 pp. 105-109.

[68] General Agreement on Tariffs and Trade. (1989) *International Trade 88-89* volumes I and II, (Geneva: GATT).

[69] General Agreement on Tariffs and Trade. (1988) "News of the Uruguay Round of Multilateral Trade Negotiations, Montreal Meeting of the Trade

Negotiations Committee, Negotiations on Trade in Services", December, (Geneva, GATT).

[70] General Agreement on Tariffs and Trade. (1986) "Ministerial Declaration on the Uruguay Round", *GATT Newsletter, Focus* 41 (Geneva: GATT), pp. 2-5.

[71] General Agreement on Tariffs and Trade. (1985) *Trade Policies for a Better Future: Proposals for Action* (Geneva: GATT).

[72] Graham, David R., Daniel P. Kaplan and David S. Sibley. (1983) "Efficiency and Competion in the Airline Industry", *Bell Journal of Economics* 14 pp. 118-138.

[73] Giaraini, Orio, (1989) "The Service Economy and the Management of Risk" in Albert Bressand and Kalypso Nicolaïdis, (eds.) (1989) *Strategic Trends in Services: An Inquiry into the Global Service Economy* (New York: Harper & Row Publishers).

[74] Giaraini, Orio, (ed.) (1987) *The Emerging Service Economy* (Oxford: Pergamon Press), for the Services World Forum, Geneva.

[75] Graham, Frank D. (1923) "Some Aspects of Protection Further Considered", *Quarterly Journal of Economics* 37 pp. 199-227

[76] Grubel, Herbert G. (1986a) "There is No Direct International Trade in Services", The Fraser Institute, Service Project Discussion Paper 86-3, mimeo.

[77] Grubel, Herbert G. (1986b) "Direct and Embodied Trade in Services", The Fraser Institute, Service Project Discussion Paper 86-1, mimeo.

[78] Grubel, Herbert G. and P. J. Lloyd. (1975) *Intra-Industry Trade: The Theory and Measurement of International Trade in Differentiated Products* (London: Macmillan).

[79] Gulati, Sunil K. and Manuel Sebastião. (1986) "Trade in Factor-Relocation-Requiring Services: A Simple Formal Model", Columbia University, mimeo.

[80] Helpman, Elhanan. (1985) "International Trade in Differentiated Middle Products", in K. G. Jungenfelt and D. Hague, eds. *Structural Adjustment in Developed Open Economies* (London: Macmillan).

[81] Helpman, Elhanan. (1981) "International Trade in the Presence of Product Differentiation, Economies of Scale and Monopolistic Competition: A Chamberlain-Heckscher-Ohlin Approach", *Journal of International Economics* 11 pp. 305-340.

[82] Helpman, Elhanan and Paul R. Krugman. (1989) *Trade Policy and Market Structure* (Cambridge, MA: The MIT Press).

[83] Helpman, Elhanan and Paul R. Krugman. (1985) *Market Structure and Foreign Trade: Increasing Returns, Imperfect Competition, and the International Economy* (Cambridge, MA: The MIT Press).

[84] Herman, B. and B. van Holst. (1981) "Towards a Theory of International Trade in Services", Foundations of Empirical Economic Research paper 1981/19, Netherlands Economic Institute, Rotterdam.

[85] Hill, T. P. (1987) "The Economic Significance of the Distinction Between Goods and Services", presented at the Twentieth General Conference of the International Association for Research in Income and Wealth, Rocca di Papa, Italy, 23-39 August, mimeo.

[86] Hill, T. P. (1977) "On Goods and Services", *Review of Income and Wealth* Series 23 pp. 315-338.

[87] Hindley, Brian. (1987) "Protection in the Service Sector: Methods and Effects", unpublished memo, preliminary draft obtained in the GATT library.

[88] Hindley, Brian. (1986) "Introducing Services into the GATT", paper prepared for the European meeting on the position of the European Community in the New GATT Round convened by the Spanish Ministry of Finance and the Economy and the Trade Policy Research Centre, Residencia Fuente Pizarro, Collado-Villalba, Spain, October 2-4.

[89] Hindley, Brian and Alasdair Smith. (1984) "Comparative Advantage and Trade in Services", *The World Economy* 7 pp. 369-389.

[90] Inman, Robert P. (ed.) (1985) *Managing the Service Economy: Prospects and Problems* (Cambridge: Cambridge University Press).

[91] International Air Transport Association. (1987) *IATA Role in International Scheduled Air Transport* (Geneva: IATA).

[92] International Air Transport Association. (1986a) *World Air Transport Statistics 1985*, number 30, WATS 6/86, (Geneva: IATA).

[93] International Air Transport Association. (1986b) *Deregulation Watch Third Report: A Report by a Group of Experts Brought Together by the International Air Transport Association* (Geneva: IATA).

[94] International Air Transport Association. (1985) *Deregulation Watch Consolidated Report: A Report by a Group of Experts Brought Together by the International Air Transport Association* (Geneva: IATA).

[95] International Air Transport Association. (1984) *Aviation Deregulation Synopsis: U. S. Domestic Deregulation Concepts and Their Potential Application to International Aviation* (Geneva: IATA).

[96] International Air Transport Association. (1983) *Aviation Deregulation: U. S. Domestic Deregulation Concepts and Their Potential Application to International Aviation* (Geneva: IATA).

[97] International Civil Aviation Organization. (1986a) *Financial Data: Commercial Air Carriers 1985* Series F-No.39, Digest of Statistics No. 331, (Montreal: ICAO).

[98] International Civil Aviation Organization. (1986b) *Financial Data: Commercial Air Carriers 1984* Series F-No.38, Digest of Statistics No. 320, (Montreal: ICAO).

[99] International Civil Aviation Organization. (1986c) *Traffic by Flight Stage 1985* Series TF-No.100, Digest of Statistics No. 333, (Montreal: ICAO).

[100] International Civil Aviation Organization. (1980) *Convention on International Civil Aviation, signed at Chicago on 7 December 1944*, 6th edition, ICAO Doc. 7300/6.

[101] International Monetary Fund. (1977) *Balance of Payments Manual* fourth edition, (Washington, D. C.: IMF).

[102] James Capel House. (1986) *International Airlines* (London: James Capel House).

[103] Jenks, Craig. (1986) "U.S. Airlines Hubs and Spokes: Developing Hubs to Dominate Market Shares", *Travel & Tourism Analyst* August, pp. 29-42.

[104] Johnson, Richard L. (1985) "Networking and Market Entry in the Airline Industry: Some Early Evidence from Deregulation", *Journal of Transport Economics and Policy* 19 pp. 299-304.

[105] Jones, Ronald W. and Henryk Kierzkowski. (1988) "The Role of Services in Production and International Trade: A Theoretical Framework" April, unpublished mimeo.

[106] Jones, Ronald W. and Frances Ruane (1988) "Appraising the Options for International Trade in Services" March, unpublished mimeo.

[107] Joy, Stewart. (1986) "Contestable Market Analysis in the Australian Domestic Airline Industry", *Journal of Transport Economics and Policy* 20 pp. 245-254.

[108] Kahn, Alfred E. (1988) "Surprises of Airline Deregulation", *The American Economic Review: AEA Papers and Proceedings* 78 pp. 316-322.

[109] Kahn, Alfred E. (1982) "Is It Time to Re-regulate the Airline Industry?", *The World Economy* 5 pp. 341-360.

[110] Kahn, Alfred E. (1988) *The Economics of Regulation: Principles and Institutions, (volume one: Economic Principles, and volume two: Institutional Issues)* a reprint of the 1970-71 volumes, (Cambridge, MA: The MIT Press).

[111] Kasper, Daniel M. (1987) "Trade Liberalization in Air Services: How to Get There from Here", presented at the "Trade in Services and the Uruguay Rund Negotiations" conference sponsored by the Centre for Applied Studies in International Negotiations, Geneva; the Trade Policy Research Centre, London; and the American Enterprise Institute, Washington, D. C. 10 July, (forthcoming).

[112] Katouzian, M. A. (1970) "The Development of the Service Sector: A New Approach", *Oxford Economic Papers* 22 pp. 362-382.

[113] Keeler, Theodore E. (1989) "Airline Deregulation and Market Performance: The Economic Basis for Regulatory Reform and Lessons from the U.S. Experience", Working Paper No. 89-123, University of California at Berkeley.

[114] Kierzkowski, Henryk. (1987a) "Recent Advances in International Trade Theory: A Selective Survey", *Oxford Review of Economic Policy* 3 pp 1-19.

[115] Kierzkowski, Henryk. (1987b) "International Trade in Services and Deregulation of Domestic Markets", The Graduate Institute of International Studies, Geneva, mimeo.

[116] Kierzkowski, Henryk. (1986) "Modeling International Transportation Services", International Monetary Fund Research Department paper DM/86/35.

[117] Kierzkowski, Henryk, (ed.) (1984a) *Monopolistic Competition and International Trade* (Oxford: Clarendon Press).

[118] Kierzkowski, Henryk. (1984b) "Services in the Development Process and Theory of International Trade", Discussion Papers in International Economics, No. 8405, (Geneva: The Graduate Institute of International Studies).

[119] Kierzkowski, Henryk and André Sapir. (1987) "International Trade in Services: Perspectives From the Developing Countries", extracts from an unpublished mimeo.

[120] Kim, H. Youn. (1987) "Economies of Scale in Multi-product Firms: an Empirical Analysis", *Economica* 54 pp. 185-206.

[121] Kim, H. Youn. (1986) "Economies of Scale and Economies of Scope in Multiproduct Financial Institutions: Further Evidence from Credit Unions" *Journal Of Money, Credit and Banking* 18 pp. 220-226.

[122] Koten, John. (1987) "Non-U.S. Airlines Face Flap on Domestic American Trips", *The Wall Street Journal* 8 December, p. 5.

[123] Krommenacker, Raymond J. (1984) *World-Traded Services: The Challenge for the Eighties* (Dedham, MA: Artech House).

[124] Krugman, Paul. (1984) "Import Protection as Export Promotion: International Competition in the Presence of Oligopoly and Economies of Scale" in Henryk Kierzkowski (ed.) (1984) *Monopolistic Competition and International Trade* (Oxford: Clarendon Press).

[125] Krugman, Paul. (1979) "Increasing Returns to Scale, Monopolistic Competition, and International Trade", *Journal of International Economics* 9 pp. 469-479.

[126] Lall, Sanjaya. (1982) "Trade in Services and Development", Oxford University, mimeo.

[127] Lancaster, Kelvin. (1979) *Variety, Equity and Efficiency* (New York: Columbia University Press).

[128] Lanvin, Bruno. (1989) "Information, Services and Development: Some Conceptual and Analytical Issues" in Albert Bressand and Kalypso Nicolaïdis (eds.) (1989) *Strategic Trends in Services: An Inquiry into the Global Service Economy* (New York: Harper & Row Publishers).

[129] Lanvin, Bruno. (1988) "Services intermédiares et dévloppement", *Revue d'Economie Industrielle*, Special issue: Le dynamisme des services aux entreprises, No. 43, Paris, 1st Semester.

[130] Lawrence, Colin. (1989) "Banking Costs, Generalized Functional Forms, and Estimation of Economies of Scale and Scope", *Journal of Money, Credit, and Banking* 21 pp. 368-79.

[131] Lazar, Fred. (1989) "Airline Deregulation: A Footnote on the Missing Entrants", *Australian Economic Papers* December pp. 246-52.

[132] Markusen, James. (1986a) "Trade in Producer Services: Issues Involving Returns to Scale, and the International Division of Labour", The Institute for Research on Public Policy, Victoria, Canada, Discussion Paper Series on Trade in Services, December.

[133] Markusen, James. (1986b) "Trade in Producer Services: Issues Involving Agglomeration Economies, Human Capital and Public Inputs", The Insti-

tute for Research on Public Policy, Victoria, Canada, Discussion Paper Series on Trade in Services, December.

[134] McGowan, Francis and Chris Trengrove. (1986) *European Aviation: A Common Market?* IFS report series No. 23, (London: The Institute for Fiscal Studies).

[135] Melvin, James R. (1987a) "Services: Dimensionality and Intermediation in Economic Analysis" The Institute for Research on Public Policy, Victoria, Canada, Discussion Paper Series on Trade in Services, January.

[136] Melvin, James R. (1987b) "Trade in Services: A Heckscher-Ohlin Approach" The Institute for Research on Public Policy, Victoria, Canada, Discussion Paper Series on Trade in Services, January.

[137] Mester, Loretta J. (1987) "A Multiproduct Cost Study of Savings and Loans" *Journal of Finance* 42 pp. 423-445.

[138] Mitchell, Mark L. and Michael T. Maloney (1989) "Crisis in the Cockpit? The Role of Market Forces in Promoting Air Travel Safety", *Journal of Law and Economics* 32 pp. 329-55.

[139] Moore, Thomas G. (1986) "U.S. Airline Deregulation: Its Effects on Passengers, Capital, and Labor", *Journal of Law and Economics* 29 pp. 1-28.

[140] Morrison, Steven and Clifford Winston. (1989) " Enhancing the Performance of the Deregulated Air Transportation System", *Brookings Papers on Economic Activity*, (Microeconomic Issue), pp. 61-123.

[141] Morrison, Steven and Clifford Winston. (1987) "Empirical Implications and Tests of the Contestability Hypothesis", *Journal of Law and Economics* 30 pp. 53-66.

[142] Morrison, Steven and Clifford Winston. (1986) *The Economic Effects of Airline Deregulation* (Washington, D. C.: The Brookings Institution).

[143] Mundell, Robert A. (1957) "International Trade and Factor Mobility", *American Economic Review* 47 pp. 321-335.

[144] de Murias, Ramon. (1989) *The Economic Regulation of International Air Transport* (Jefferson, North Carolina: McFarland & Company, Inc., Publishers).

[145] Nayyar, Deepak. (1989) "Towards a Possible Multilateral Framework for Trade in Services: Some Issues and Concepts", a report prepared for the United Nations Conference on Trade and Development, UNCTAD/ITP/17, October 4, (New York: United Nations Publications).

[146] Norman, Victor D. and Siri P. Strandenes (1990) "Deregulation of Scandinavian Airlines: A Case of Study of the Oslo-Stockholm Route", Discussion Paper Series No. 403, (London: Centre for Economic Policy Research).

[147] Nusbaumer, Jacques. (1987a) *Services in the Global Market* (Boston: Kluwer Academic Publishers).

[148] Nusbaumer, Jacques. (1987b) *The Services Economy: Lever to Growth* (Boston: Kluwer Academic Publishers).

[149] Nusbaumer, Jacques. (1986) "Les Négociations Internationales sur les Services ou la Quadrature du Cercle" *Revue d'Économie Politique* 5 pp. 541-550.

[150] Nusbaumer, Jacques. (1985) "Services and the International Economic Agenda" *International Geneva 1985* Centre for Research on International Institutions (Lausanne: Payot).

[151] Nusbaumer, Jacques. (1984) "Some Implications of Becoming a Service Economy" in Rada, J. F. and G. R. Pipe eds., *Communication Regulation and International Business* (Amsterdam: Elsevier Science Publishers B. V.).

[152] Organization for Economic Co-operation and Development. (1989) *Trade in Services and Developing Countries* (Paris: OECD).

[153] Organization for Economic Co-operation and Development. (1988) *Deregulation and Airline Competition* (Paris: OECD).

[154] Panzar, John C. and Robert D. Willig. (1981) "Economies of Scope", *American Economic Review: AEA Papers and Proceedings* 71 pp. 268-272.

[155] Peltzman, Sam. (1989) "The Economic Theory of Regulation after a Decade of Deregulation", *Brookings Papers on Economic Activity*, (Microeconomic Issue), pp. 1-59.

[156] Petit, Pascal. (1987) "Internationalization of Services and New Forms of Competition", paper presented at the Sixth International conference of Europeanists, Washington, October 30-November 1.

[157] Pindyck, Robert S. and Daniel L. Rubinfeld (1981) *Econometric Models and Economic Forecasts* second edition, (Auckland: McGraw-Hill International Book Company).

[158] Pryke, Richard. (1987) *Competiton Among International Airlines* Thames Essay No. 46, (London: Trade Policy Research Centre).

[159] Reid, S. R. and J. W. Mohrfeld. (1973) "Airline Size, Profitability, Mergers and Regulation", *Journal of Air Law and Commerce* 39 pp. 167-178.

[160] Reiss, Peter and Pablo T. Spiller (1989) "Competition and Entry in Small Airline Markets", *Journal of Law and Economics* supplement pp. S179-S202.

[161] Richardson, John B. (1987) "A Sub-sectoral Approach to Services' Trade Theory", in Orio Giarini, ed. *The Emerging Service Economy* (Oxford: Pergamon Press).

[162] Riddle, Dorothy I. (1986) *Service-Led Growth: The Role of the Service Sector in World Development* (New York: Praeger Publishers).

[163] Sampson, Gary P. and R. H. Snape. (1985) "Identifying the Issues in Trade in Services", *The World Economy* 8 pp. 171-181.

[164] Sapir, André. (1985) "North-South Issues in Trade in Services", *The World Economy* 8 pp. 27-42.

[165] Sapir, André and E. Lutz. (1981) "Trade in Services: Economic Determinants and Development Related Issues", *World Bank Staff Working Paper No. 480* (Washington, D. C.: The World Bank).

[166] Sapir, André and E. Lutz. (1980) "Trade in Non-factor Services: Past Trends and Current Issues", *World Bank Staff Working Paper No. 410* (Washington, D. C.: The World Bank).

[167] Sawers, David. (1987) *Competion in the Air: What Europe Can Learn from the USA* IEA research monograph No. 41, (London: The Institute of Economic Affairs).

[168] Schott, Jeffrey J. and Jacqueline Meza. (1986) "Trade in Services and Developing Countries", *Journal of World Trade Law* 6 pp. 195-214.

[169] Shepherd, William G. (1984) " 'Contestability' vs. Competition", *American Economic Review* 74 pp. 572-587.

[170] Spero, Joan E. (1990) "Trade in Services: Achilles Heel of the G.A.T.T. Negotiations?", presented at conference on "Uruguay Round Negotiations:

The Last Lap", convened by the Royal Institute of International Affairs and the Trade Policy Research Centre, London, January 18.

[171] Spiller, Pablo T. (1989) "A Note on Pricing of Hub-and-Spoke Networks", *Economic Letters* 30 pp. 165-69.

[172] Spulber, Daniel F. (1989) *Regulation and Markets* (Cambridge, MA: The MIT Press).

[173] Stern, Robert M. (1984) "Global Dimensions and Determinants of International trade and Investment in Services", paper presented at the Third Annual Workshop on US-Canadian Relations, 19-20 October.

[174] Straszheim, Mahion R. (1969) *The International Airline Industry* (Washington, D. C.: The Brookings Institution).

[175] Tucker, Ken and Mark Sundberg. (1986) "Comparative Advantage and Service Intensity in Traded Goods", *ASEAN-Australia Economic Papers No. 23* (Kuala Lumpur and Canberra: ASEAN-Australia Joint Research Project).

[176] United Nations Conference on Trade and Development. (1988) *Services* TD/B/1162, (New York: United Nations Publications).

[177] United Nations Conference on Trade and Development. (1985) *Services and the Development Process* TD/B/1008/Rev.1, (New York: United Nations Publications).

[178] Vanek, Jaroslav. (1968) "Factor Proportions Theory: The N-Factor Case", *Kyklos* 24 pp.749-56.

[179] Weisman, Ethan. (1990) *Trade in Services and Imperfect Competition* thesis presented at the University of Geneva, *Institut Universitaire de Hautes Études Internationales*, to obtain the title of *Docteur ès sciences politiques*, thesis No. 461, (Geneva: *Imprimerie Nationale*)

[180] Weisman, Ethan. (1983) *Cooperative Development: The Potential in Eastern Africa* M. A. thesis, Department of Economics, The University of Texas at Austin.

[181] Wellington, Arthur M. (1887) *The Economic Theory of the Location of the Railways* (New York: John Wiley & Sons).

[182] White, Lawrence J. (1979) "Economies of Scale and the Question of 'Natural Monopoly' in the Airline Industry", *Journal of Air Law and Commerce* 44 pp. 545-573.

[183] Winston, Clifford. (1985) "Conceptual Developments in the Economics of Transportation: An Interpretive Survey", *Journal of Economic Literature* 33 pp. 57-94.

[184] World Bank. (1987) *World Development Report 1987* (New York: Oxford University Press)

[185] Zweifel, Peter. (1986) "On the Tradeability of Services", paper presented to the Third Annual PROGRES Seminar on the Service Economy, Geneva, 2-3 June.